translated by

查利伍

chá lì wǔ
charlie5

pentamagical@gmail.com

Translator's Preface

Ling Bao Daoism is a 5th century Chinese philosophy that strives to teach immortality by pointing to aspects of nature, and directing us toward transcendence by contemplating the Way of Heaven.

In "Primal Beginning Boundless Salvation Highest Level Mystical Scripture, 元始無量度人上品妙經", a central Ling Bao Daoism treatise, immortality is pointed toward by several phrases meant to direct us into a sense of wonder.

The sun, a "projection" that revolves, is the "golden precious carriage of immortality", an "immortal phoenix" that "coils around the dense growth of passions and delusions below", is a motif that relies on the patterns of the sky over our world as a "river of immortality" to teach us about the Dao, the "Path", the "Way of Heaven", as a sort of orientation class.

The idea of "Primal Heaven's Salvation" is that we awaken to our immortality, the "secret truth of our ancestors", flying away from our mundane lives into a life more like that of the stars, into a mind that is quiet, simple, and pure, rising like the sun into the sky, steadily, "ascending in fullness and peace" into a Heaven that is pure clarity, the "eternally flowing river of immortality", in a "festival of salvation" that reaches the "other shore", "beyond the three borders of Past, Present, and Future existence", "stepping into the ripening that attains the seat of immortality", "flying above the three borders to win the beyond";

In Ling Bao Daoism the universe is like a bible, a YIN and YANG map on the sky that is always moving, "growing in learning knots and slowly flowing tears" that are the stars, a universe whose "external manifestation" is the three borders of Past, Present, and Future existence, "ripening in the soaring of time, ascending, guided by the imperial pilot through the cloud gate and into the quiet clarity of Heaven"; "the immortal in the great deep pool of blue-green swims as if in a river of perpetual dawn"

Two lines from a famous Chinese poem about immortality -

龍湖鼎鼎
丹竈珠流

*"At Dragon Lake, the cauldron has disappeared;
in the cinnabar furnace, pearls flow"*

The sage saves the universe by saving the universe inside himself; for the Buddha, immortal, the universe is the lake, the outer ring of the mandala that is the Buddha, and is the dragon, and the lake is his home, his to take care of, to cultivate, to relieve from suffering into truth, the happiness beyond birth and death. Ascending to the perspective of immortality, the physical universe becomes "Dragon Lake", and the saha world that was a "cauldron" of suffering is transformed by the simple change of perspective into the "cinnabar furnace", cinnabar being the traditional Daoist elixir of immortality; the entire universe and its calendar are an opportunity to be grateful for, the furnace where immortality is brewed; without the inner nine circles there wouldn't be a tenth, outer circle of Buddha; "pearls flow" is part of the phrase "pearls flow, jade moves on", figurative for water under the bridge, the jade being the universe, the pearls being the stars, their movement being the Yin of Heaven, the phrase encouraging us to just let it happen, not to add to it and not to worry about it; no suffering, only pearls flowing in eternity.

The tree of life is the crown on the altar of reality, and we all contribute to the flourishing of that tree, no matter which of the ten worlds we find ourselves in; the thin roots go out into the soil of the real, and above, the leaves cover the branches; this is our life in the world, working, taking care of ourselves, tending to our gardens in time, all contributing to the leaves on the tree of life; then there are the deeper roots of spiritual practice, penetrating deep beyond the soil of the real to the underground river of immortality, to the divine, into eternity, and offering the tree another kind of nourishment that the soil of the real could never provide, and high up on the tree of life, it is as a result of the nourishment from these deep tap roots, that the flowers of joy and the fruits of prayers of compassion-happiness grow, the peaches of immortality.

When I started reading the Ling Bao Daoist scriptures and began to understand their vision, I realized the Dao isn't the path we're "supposed" to take, it's that path that IS, it's the 萬遍道, "wàn biàn dào " - the "10,000 everywheres" Dao; it's the Way of Heaven, not theist but monist; it's not the universe but the flow of the universe is its symbol; the Way of Heaven, the path of the stars. I twist and turn in the River of Way - I work for the universe, I have a contract, to carry the universe toward the universe, by means of the universe; monist, the "I" in that statement is Heaven, 總御 - zǒng yù - focused bundle, heaven and man, progressing smoothly on the long flowing anti river of immortality; solemn and reverent, form peaceful and lovely in silent and profound obscurity; (bundle focused, it is nondual, 'all-inclusive self-envisionment', everything is the self, nothing is anything else, nothing to crave; driving straight down the hallway of the apparent, resistant to the flow of the fluid mandala of knowable things);

The Dao is as indefinable yet simple as the path of clouds across the sky, like the path of Heaven and Earth, the path of immortality, suspended in the six harmonies - *[wú wàng - not being forgetful or in error, wú xiǎng - without thought or longing, wú běn - having no root or stem, wú yuán - passive and without a source, wú tǐ - having no body or substance, wú lèi - without clinging or involvement]*.

"The white sun rises into Heaven, its flying star-steps a summoning dance through the hollow void, body born of fire and water in a magical transformation of nothing into forever, its heavenly immortality of truth a single-minded hope alone in his dragon womb of liquid gold, cinnabar elixir of the nine transforming revolutions...."

(白日升天飛步虛空身生水火變化無常其天仙之真唯有龍胎金液九轉之丹)

- from the Book of the Five Talismans 五符經 wǔ fú jīng (Taishang lingbao wufu jing 太上靈寶五符經) - (DZ 388)
[http://ctext.org/library.pl?if=gb&file=99014&page=163]

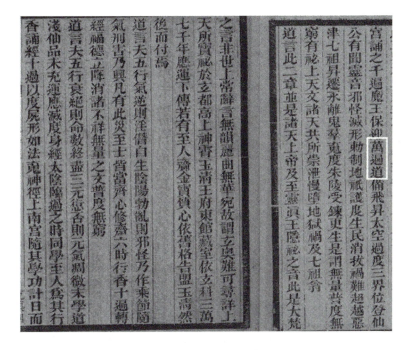

迎萬遍道備昇太空過度三界位登仙公有聞
靈音邪怪滅形勅制地祇護度生民消拔禍難
超越惡津七祖昇遷永離鬼羣冤度朱陵受鍊
更生寔謂無量普度無窮有祕上天文諸天

"to face and to welcome the "WAN BIAN DAO" - the "ten thousand everywheres" Dao - in preparation to rise and to ascend in fullness and peace like the sunrise into the Great Emptiness, the Great Vacant Vacuity, into the Spirit above illusory existence, the abstraction without relativity, transgression and error fallen away into the Past, in a celebration of crossing over, the festival of salvation that reaches the other shore, beyond the three borders of Past, Present, and Future Existence, stepping into the ripening that attains the seat of immortality, awakening into the secret truth of the ancestors and kings that exists when hearing the efficacious spirit sounds that extinguish and defeat the mysterious evils, blowing out the bewildering flame that leads toward error and illness; the body's form absorbing the powerful imperial commands to simmer in regulation and restraint, while reverent earth spirits protect the inner self as well as the body, saving the life of the people, the elder brother of poetry melting and wiping away misfortune, pulling up disaster and calamity by the roots, leaping over distress to pass into bliss, crossing over beyond the prison of evil that tries to trap the Qi, riding the ferry of salvation to the seven founding ancestors in a peaceful ascent that swims in the eternally flowing brightness of immortality, leaving behind the flock of hungry ghosts and scattered wandering dreams, and crossing over to the vermilion mountains and rose sky of the fairy realm, to receive-accept-endure the refinement, the training that holds the wind of experience contained within to receive the blessings of Heaven and earth, standing in the middle of the boat with both hands open to bear, and going further, into pure life; this is truly called the boundless and inexhaustible universal salvation, the mysterious secret of ascending into Heaven"

- the Wan Bian Dao - from "Numinous Treasure Primal Beginning Boundless Salvation Highest Level Mystical Scripture " (Líng Bǎo Wú Liáng Dù Rén Shàng Pǐn Miào Jīng -靈寶元始無量度人上品妙經) (DZ 5) scroll 53

So we're all a part of the Dao, because we have bodies in the world. So what isn't the Dao? The netherworld of the human mind, a Maya that doesn't exist. At best it's a mirror of the Dao, bright and linked in heaven's harmony. Otherwise its darkness and confusion Is simply unreal, and not the Dao.

```
大         身至縱行時為大         大
道         也無身或是坐無道         道
無         此為如立或所喻         無
為         言是大任或施人         為
           卻人空氣臥為身
           破無始胎或也無
                 息    身
                      也
```

大道無為大道喻人身無為是無所施為也時或坐或臥或行或立任氣胎息縱身如大空始至無為是人無身也此言卻破大道無為
- DaoZang Volume 131, Page 090a2
http://www.dztranslation.org/texts/vol-0131/daozang-0131-090a2.html

"The Great Dao is wu-wei; the Great Way can be described with analogy/metaphor/allegory as man's self in non-action; there's no 'place to carry out action; at times perhaps to sit, lie down, walk, or stand up, to allow the Qi to flow naturally; to give free reign to the Qi, allowing it to breathe, rest, stop, settle, and cease, and be an embryo, body released, as if it is in the Great empty vacant void; it begins with perfect wu-wei, to be a man with no body; this is to say that – breaking, disrupting, solving, negating, getting rid of and defeating is done via the Great Way – wu wei"

"The Great Dao is non-action".

There's such a thing as 無為 "wu-wei", prayer for prayer, not for the purpose of something; in Daoism they call it "the highest vehicle".

There's also a distinction to be made, I think, about prayer; the prayer of the shaman who prays "I love you!" isn't doing that for a payoff, not trying to bring the numinous back into the netherworld of human life; it's wu-wei, not for the purpose of something; there is a purpose, but it's not something; it's the irrationality of spiritual practice, the prayer as its own goal.

The author of "The Universe is Calling" quotes Master Eckhart describing our waking life as something to be 'woken up' from, to emerge from a "sensual and materialistic" consciousness into something more silent and deep.

I tend to phrase the same idea with the opposite imagery, where wakeful life is the materialistic and sensual distraction, the Maya of delusion, and in the silence of sleep, the "mysterious receptacle of stillness", we dream as we pray, as Jesus did on the rough seas while his apostles were frightened, as Han Xiang Zi the second of the eight Daoist immortals did while he did his prayer for snow; our waking life is like clear water, a place where we work together in a shared consciousness of clarity in the light of day, but when we sleep the consciousness is not only more private, but less like water and more like caramel, and it's the caramel that touches the difference, the depth of divinity. And in Ling Bao Daoism they call the stillness-as-prayer the "highest vehicle", and use the word "wu-wei", (無爲), sometimes translated simply as not-doing but more appropriately as "doing but not for the purpose of something"; there is a purpose, but it's not something, the divine, inscrutable purpose, like the sun, the moon, and the wind, shining, going out, and disappearing.

In Sanskrit the same concept is called "nihitartho" -

(from verse 4.1 of the SvetaSvata Upanishad, describing the purpose of creating the universe)

In the Bhagavad Gita, the hero is told: "Look around you; other than action for the purpose of sacrifice, all men are constrained to action; therefore, act "not for the purpose of something".

"Wu wei", non-action, is the doing of spiritual exercise, of spiritual practice, the doing of mental, physical, and spiritual fasting; it's slow, prolonged, and mindful breathing - "pranayama" - and the doing of yoga - a union with the universe - it's standing in the steelyard of heaven where the gold of the stars is refined, under heat and pressure, where the YANG is brought out and then put to bed on fixed schedule, the language of heaven a rhythm; rather than the misunderstanding that it is not doing anything, I use the phrase "marching forward in the snowfall of non-action" to point out the effort and the accomplishment of wu-wei, the stillness in the jade hailstorm of modernity, of a tranquility worker immersed in tranquility craft, because it is the adding of numinous energy into the system, rather than letting the system attract to its lowest energy state, and in the mysterious receptacle of stillness the magic of life accumulates, in "shou", 受, receive-accept-endure, yoga at the center of the storm, the light of eternity shining through the opaque rustling of the existential; we step out onto the jade flower of truth, placing ourselves fully onto the altar of reality by mindfully filling ourselves with "wu-wei".

"With a simple move the Green jade is inhabited" (俯仰碧居), the "Jade flower" that is the blossoming cavity, the heaven all around us, the altar of reality, the snowflake at the center of the outwardly blossoming "primal profound"- "anterior heaven", and with the small step of a "simple move" we can come up out of a netherworld that doesn't exist, that can't be found on this altar of reality, and we come up to "shou" 受 ('receive-accept-endure') the tidings of primal heaven, the great transformation that falls universally, rather than hiding from it in the dark netherworld; we can cover ourselves with smoking and eating and drinking and entertainment like an umbrella in the divine rain, or we can learn to walk out into the rain in an act of love for the universe, accepting the gift of transformation and moving forward on the path, together on a string, sitting on a frontier of magic and deathlessness.

"Fú Yǎng Bì Jū
With a simple move the Green Jade becomes inhabited."
http://dztranslation.org/texts/vol-0005/daozang-0005-037b1.html

The "green jade" is the altar of reality we find standing before us when we escape from the prison of the netherworld that is the occupation of our hearts and minds in the modern world, it's the blue-green 'raw' jade, standing in the sunshine of the true Self, with a door below, deep within the earth, to the netherworld; it is the verdant greenery of our world of life, but also the blue sky, the opalescent and nacreous clouds, a green that's iridescent with the colors of the five directions shimmering in the pneuma of the sun, and it extends to all of the heavens above; it is the grand rectificatory and purificatory fluid ocean of "Qi" 氣 that we exist in, all pneuma, the marvelous numinous spiritual energy howling in the wind and rain through the thatched windows, and in the dance of the shaman, the green fluid charm of verdant created fortune, bright, clear, and awe-inspiring green brilliance, the "Grand Green Flower", a 'blossoming cavity of wonderful emptiness', and as the netherworld empties, the brilliance returns to the Jade.

The "netherworld" is obscure and remote, hidden away, a prison, a dark and deep underworld, profound, secret, and invisible, a world of ignorance, as opposed to being open and manifest 顯 (xian). "There is Heaven above and what is beneath Heaven, and bottomless and hidden beneath is the netherworld 无幽 (wu you), without form or contrast 无冥 (wu ying), without shadow, image, or reflection 无影 (wu ying)." And this is what we step out of to inhabit the Green Jade.

The divine spirit energy, that the king of demons 魔王 "Mo Wang" wants to convert, to steal, to make the tidings of Heaven a part of his netherworld. Instead of being confined in his prison, the adept rises up with the heart and mind to form an "alliance with heaven" 盟天 "meng tian", "tossing away concerns that never really existed" (擲罔奠斯 Zhì Wǎng Diàn Sī), the 'feelings' of heart and mind in the netherworld tossed away as we step out onto the jade flower of truth, placing ourselves fully onto the altar of reality by mindfully filling ourselves with 無爲 "wu-wei" ("non-action"), marching forward in the snowfall of non-action, and going out into the blossoming emptiness, all kindness and the energy of truth and good fortune in the void of dark mystery. "The spiritual power in the omen of green is venerated with reverence." (靈兆绿敬 Líng Zhào Lú Jìng Tiān).

It's a change in perspective, away from the "netherworld" of the mind of man, with its immediate desires, its confusion, the materialist culture, so separate as it is from the universe, from the "Dao", and suggesting a "simple, single move", from looking "down", into that netherworld, where all the science and reason are, to looking "up", into the sky, past the clouds, through the heavens, toward the origins, the beginning of time, toward our ancestors, and encouraging us to take their perspective, and then on looking back into the daily existence of our world, to carry them forward within us as they might have hoped and expected, from "up there"; it's like the Catholic concept of the "crowd of witnesses", cheering us on as we make our decisions. Would they want us to let go of God, to be more "independent", all hubris within our limited netherworld, the mud of our mundane and material mind, the burning acidic pool, the hot springs of the lost-in-thought self-absorption? Or to look up, to let the Garden of Eden that is the universe all around us nurture us on our path as we walk with divinity in a glorious festival of salvation?

It's not about personal subjectivity, no splendor to be "gotten", even if that's what modern culture is preaching; the place to look for the salvation in this vision is in the transcendental, it's the subjectivity of the universe itself, as a single, unified, living thing.

What we 'are' is not our mind, not our subjectivity, that's only an outer layer, something we 'live in', just like we are not our clothes or our homes, we are not our feelings, our consciousness, rather, under the pressure and in the coat of 'Maya', the world of illusion, our minds are a netherworld, a dream, and what we really are tends, in this society of western materialism, to go running down the drain into that netherworld. But there is another "Way".

The jade flower of heaven all around us is the host; the dark netherworld of ordinary heart and mind is the guest; the guest draws abstract art on a palette of netherworld nothingness, it's a palette that all species have but few mine to the extent that humanity does, humanity a species poisoned somehow and dropping depth charges of more stimulants and poisons daily to continue to expand a nothingness that captures the precious "prana" of Hindu mysticism, the "itz" of the Mayan religion, the "Qi" of Daoism, the manna from heaven, as it rains down in blessed tidings from the primal heaven above, from redshift space, above the jade flower. But if we make that "simple move" out of the netherworld and "inhabit the jade", become a part of the universe and keep the door closed to the netherworld, the tidings can pile up here on the altar of reality, and not run down the drain, and this critical piece of magic is in our hands, and it's not in the hands of consciousness, that's the netherworld already, it's in the hands of spirit.

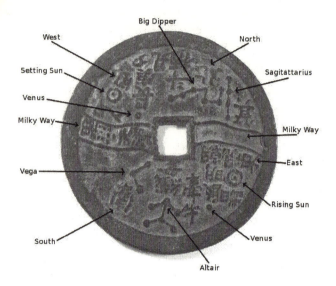

Not taught to cultivate life, we hurtle toward death, the "attractors" hurled at us from every direction in the jade hailstorm of stress that is the modern world, the cloud of locusts that swarms the human condition always pushing the spring of numinosity down the drain into the netherworld, the "attractor" of stability that is the isolation and desolation of addiction, but also the netherworld of television watching, shopping, gambling, the "hundred energies", the modern storm of locusts; but the beautiful sounds of teaching that rear and nourish into the perfection of pure life are the attractors on the other end of the spectrum, hidden in our modern world, but available to the sleuth, the seeker of truth; they teach us to add numinous energy to the system in the form of stillness, to simmer in regulation and restraint, with the doing of the self – "wei shen"; 為身, with 'one's own power to accomplish saving, one's own power to accomplish calm quiescence, "zi cheng"; 自成.

What becomes of consciousness when we've flowed up out of the netherworld of our waking mind of consensual reality to inhabit the jade beautiful flower?

"The remote and hidden away rises up and becomes manifest like the sun rising, and the spirit energy responds, to be reflected on and studied, followed and complied with, the heart and mind moved, skillfully surrendering into an auspicious and felicitous amalgamation with virtue" (幽顯神靈應念隨心感善降祥與德); "accordant kindness, gracious favor and benefit are what remains, gathering into our form and accumulating, storing up in the depths of inner strength and profundity " (惠余正蘊); "surrendering to the real summons the marvelous numinous spiritual energy" (降眞召靈) and "the teaching of the universe falls like leaves, settling onto the bamboo mat where we sit" (教筵宙落), "the universe falling and settling onto us for the great transformation" (普落大化), "the positive beauty of change", "the benefit is an elegant and beautiful display of bright shining divine positive beautiful transformation and metamorphosis" (惠正麗變), and "all obtain the revolving fortune of salvation within their nature to comprehend, perceive, and awaken to truth, tranquil content and calm while guarding and protecting the emptiness" (皆得運度性悟眞空安鎭).

Surrendered to the unfathomable flow, crossing the ocean of mundane existence, samsara, the "saha world" 娑婆世界, with the radiance of transparent mystery, transforms to make one's virtue bright and eradicate obstructions; form emerging from the square, blessings out into the air, treasure gleaming, mind aware, no more netherworldly care;

I also find the Hindu Upanishads, the "Vedantic" wisdom, making the same points.

The simple way I try to put the point about 'pursuing happiness' is that my role is more like that of the sun, and my feelings like the flowers on the earth – the point of the sun is to shine, not to grow flowers; as a result of that shine, flowers will surely grow, just as surely as they will wither with the seasons, but ultimately the flowers are beside the point. What I see the sun pursuing is the "cultivation" of joy.

A 2013 article about the films directed by the philosopher Terrence Malick discusses in depth the duality suggested between the netherworld of heart/mind - the "Western world view" - and the transcendence in the green of nature - the "alternative world view of the artist", a "transcendentalist visual symphony" in which "beauty transcends history"; the Western world view of the Enlightenment that wants to "systematize and conquer nature", "it's only reality being the recognition in the minds of other men"; the simple step of looking up at the natural world and the universe all around it is the perspective of the artist, and of the camera in these films; "habits of vision characterized by ambition, skepticism, and greed" are contrasted with the "virtues of patience, appreciation and awe", the emptiness of a perspective from which a character looks like "quite an individual" contrasted with a worldview that "cannot be described in terms of what she owns or wants her desires are eccentric, fleeting, almost literally incomprehensible...yet the things she observes are finally less fanciful or obscure than in the 'realistic' perceptions of the film's other protagonists...(ultimately showing) a durability that eludes the other characters, caught up as they are in webs of aspiration and striving...not 'confined by modern civilization' her 'weak' sense of self is precisely the quality that grants her such a bracing access to a world the rest of the characters only occasionally perceive but which is inscribed by Malick as a critical, perhaps the critical, element in the story he has to tell";

> *"There may exist a perspective from which even death is a thing of beauty, the expression of some larger 'glory'. This perspective may be Witt's and it may also be that of Malick's films."*

The vision suggested in the article is one of integration of the "artistic perspective" into the "Western" one, weaving the netherworld of human heart and mind and the heaven of the Green Charm together:

"The task is not to choose between competing 'realities' but to appreciate their common root. This is the visual ethic of Malick's camera. (The movies) Days of Heaven and New Worlds denote not times and places, but a way of seeing. This way of seeing is ridiculed as sentimental and naive within the films and often by critics of them. Indeed, Malick is often described even by his proponents as a romantic or idealistic filmmaker with a tragic conception of modern life. "Each is frustrated by his insignificance or driven by a desire to become significant in the Western sense. Consequently, each fails to see the world in the manner suggested by Malick's art, instead embroiling himself in self-defeating projects supported by fantasies of entrapment or escape. To recognize these as fantasies is one of the perspecuities nourished by Malick's films."

- https://thepointmag.com/2010/criticism/the-perspective-of-terrence-malick

却守和氣
此名玄之又玄也
之法我等自入
流轉不出生死
貪瞋愚癡墮在
諸有雖福業
因緣得生天上
但清靜無為最
上乘法也

"Of the method, we awaken to and begin to understand, to become equal to; to float, flow, wander, spread, circulate, move, drift, revolve, and transform, but not to emerge into life and death, voracious anger, silly delusion, and the various kinds of degeneration, but with good fortune, blessing, and happiness to engage in the 'cause that produces effects in another stage of existence', and obtain life in heaven above."

In this mandala, made up of a phrase from "Numinous Treasure Primal Beginning Boundless Salvation Highest Level Mystical Scripture " (靈寶元始無量度人上品妙經) (DZ 5) scroll 21, that included the sentence translated above surrounded by two other sentences, the character for insanity, or "delusions", is at the center, not to radiate outward but because it is the drain that the heavenly tidings are drawn down, but if blocked off, the tidings can accumulate.

"But abiding in, guarding, and watching over the harmony of the Qi is the name for the mystery of mystery;" "Only quiescent clarity - qing jing - and non doing are the methods of the highest vehicle. " These are the outer two sentences on the mandala.

The character 癡 - 'unconsciousness,' 'delusion,' 'perplexity,' 'infatuation, 'ignorance, folly,' one of the three poisons - "desire, dislike, delusion", here occupies the center square, which, as in the previous mandalas, is the only place it can, since it doesn't actually "exist" anywhere in the jade flower, the altar of reality, but only in the netherworld of heart and mind, just an artifact of the culture of science and reason, doesn't actually 'exist' at all;

From the Hindu view, 'Maya', our consciousness of material reality in time, is an illusion - an illusion created by a god who loves us, created for our enjoyment - but still, delusion, illusion, and so 'science and reason' from this point of view is just illusion looking at illusion, completely beside the point.

Unlike the cosmic vision of modern "consensual" reality of today's industrial society, where we treat the altar of reality like a garbage heap while piling up comfort and pleasure in a netherworld that doesn't exist, and treat that netherworld as if it is the ONLY thing that exists, the vision in the "Jing Wu Liang Du Ren" is of a snowflake of consensual reality at the center of a cloud that creates it, and that is it's true "Self", from which it receives its salvation, something to integrate with rather than to compete against or ignore, something to join with, to form an alliance with. This existence is pure, elemental, natural, and filled with dark mystery - 玄 (xuan) - but we tend to ignore most of what's going on here, and treat the realm like it's a coliseum of selves, each self acting in a reality show, trying to 'win' a game based on our own choices, but the "great empty space is filled with peace and tranquility".

From the view of Daoism, the "Qi" is the magic on the air, on the wind, transcendent gift from heaven that rains down on us, and is stored in the mysterious receptacle of stillness, and makes us 'alive'; we breathe it in, that's the 'energy transfer' of 'consciousness' into our bodies, and we go with the flow, twist and turn in the river of Way, that altar of material reality just a gift for the creature that wears the universe as its costume, the altar of reality just a cardboard gift that will of course burn up, 'cause it's made of time, material reality and the consciousness of it in the netherworld of heart and mind just a beautiful dollhouse that is a distraction for play but ultimately beside the point.

From these viewpoints, "madness" is not an issue, and doesn't 'exist', just another wrinkle in the netherworld, unimportant, 'feeling' and 'thought' beside the point, the direction of these quietist thought systems being just to breathe, just to be a part of the gift for the universe, the 'problem' of "madness" just an artifact of 'science' and 'reason'; from the scientific view, deep within the jungle of illusion, humans are separate from the reality of the wholeness that is the universe, a monolithic performer in the wonder sphere, their 'thoughts' and 'feelings' supremely relevant, treating the altar of reality like a garbage pail while they decorate the altar of their feelings in the netherworld of their subjectivity, hungry to take in entertainment and comfort and pile it up in a palace that doesn't exist, their 'reason' and 'science' paramount in a play about power they perform, with comfort and isolate subjective 'happiness' the scorecard in a game they play but is impossible to 'win'.

Buddhism teaches the "four noble truths" 苦集滅道 - suffering, the cause of suffering, extinguishing suffering, and the way, or the path to extinguishing suffering, and the last character, "path", or "way", is the character "Dao", 道, as in Daoism. A Buddha has three bodies. One is the "manifest" body, in the world, the Bodhisattva working for peace in the world and the happiness of all beings. The second body is the "reward" body, the Buddha's reward for that work which is his wisdom, and the third body is the "dharma" body, the Truth that the Buddha is enlightened to. Some branches of eastern philosophy focus more on the human world, the manifest body, while others focus more on the dharma body, the mystical truth, like Ling Bao and Dzogchen.

"... to reach into the Daoist watchtower platform monastery of insight and contemplation, to arrive from the seeming into the real, to mentally enter into the truth, the one who is rare, hoped for, and admired, directs his thinking and his intention into the mystery and wonder, turning from his sensations and tastes to face upward, and to simmer in the correctness of the writings that are complex and difficult, the characters numerous, like ornaments on a horse's head, traditional Chinese characters flourishing, vigorous, and magnificent, filled with meaning wide and deep,
their prosperity abundant, lush like luxuriant vegetation in the heavenly book that achieves an end to disaster and distress, the mind wrapped in a bundle like a newborn baby, wise, clear, and bright, the truth of man protected by the words that are the tidings of Heaven, and becoming able to separate and disentangle himself into harmony in the great ascension of the heart; but there are many who do not look up, do not approach Heaven to fathom its depths, and are confused by what is above, hiding from the divine canopy and going around dazed in a lostedness below; they are not able to see what is like an ornament sitting on their heads; ah! the gathering and balancing that is possible with the humility of bowing one's head into the light of the wilderness, like a summoning decree, gathering together the divine spirits, ah! stretching beyond the Eastern mountains; at the proper time the four Qi (parental, acquired, inherited, and defense Qi), can be made warm, mild, and tender, swelling with plentitude, generous treatment radiating out like the sound of drums on the clear wind with the strength of Heaven's dark mystery and mystic wonder flowing like breeze in the emptiness to govern hearts and manage

rivers, allowing both to flow unimpeded and fluent through the brightness; holding the body in a slow masterful retreat that scrubs the mind with humility, washing away traces of turbulence in the low tide in order to reflect alone, in sincere dedication and without distraction, on the storehouse treasury that is the bright scene of the stars above the mountains, ah! the netherworld, secluded and peaceful, as the always-extending spun threads of mental states slows, to gaze on the numinous spirit energy of the nine heavens, the obscure blended mystery in the distinguished great wild, awakening to the precious jewel of the three heavens in the monastery watchtower platform, as the Emperor's garden enclosure of abundant existence that is set in motion on the divine wind brings pure life into completion in wholeness, to follow along compliantly with the greatness, calm and quiescent in order to shelter the vital essence, to see and to protect, to protect by seeing, and ascending to inspect the fires of heaven with the square pupils of the immortal, taut as a bow, to behold the flowing energy of the scripture that is like the warping stripes of the stars above the serene netherworld, that moves like wisps of smoke to evaporate distress and difficulty below, caressing with tender care the flocks of pure life that are not aware of their silk thread discipline, their chronicle of poetry above the chaos".....

http://ctext.org/library.pl?if=gb&file=99014&page=14 & 15
from Book of the Five Talismans (五符經 - wǔ fú jīng)

from the Huainanzi:

"*Ordinary things have their vanquishers, and only the Way has none; the reason why it has no vanquisher is that it has no constant shape or disposition- it turns like a wheel and endlessly, like the movement of the sun and moon; like Spring and Autumn that replace eachother, like the sun and moon with their days and nights, it reaches an end and begins again, and it brightens and dims again, but no one can grasp its periods.*"

from the Zuangzi:

"*Were you to let your mind roam in the insipid and your pneuma blend with the indifferent, go along with the nature of things, and make no room for personal desires, then all under Heaven would be governed*""

from the "Declarations of the Perfected" (Zhen Gao - DZ 1016):

"*The Mysterious Pattern comes from Heaven; take the mysterious as your pattern, grasp the Images, purify and cleanse yourself...purify your Lights in the Void so that they radiate in the five directions, cut off visual form in a wave-transformation, join your desires with the insipid, and in the hidden byways of undifferentiated space, see nothing and hear nothing.... truly Heaven has crafted your talents into clear ripples, and formed them into waves through its lofty resonances; you intend to perch your spirits in Grand Mystery, (Mystery Metropolis), rendezvous at Purple Court, and pace the vault of space; you're of a mind to be emptied of fleeting impediments and to have your nimble brush ornament an otherworldly covenant; your movements bring together the compass and square as you await convergence with the exotic realm; in stillness, while you harmoniously blend the flavors of Perfection, your exhalations generate musical tones; chewing the blossoms of the three numina (sun, moon, and stars), flowing in the reverberent harmony of virtue; stepping up to Rarefied Grove Palace, asleep atop Rarefied Grove; sparkling in the Jade Mystery; spirits roosting in order to roam in idleness, safely drink and peck in contentment without praying and hoping for a cage.*"

Yuanshi Tianzun -元始天尊- "Celestial Venerable of the Primordial Beginning", the highest personality in the LingBao Daoism, is the legendary source of the 5th century LingBao scripture "Du Ren Jing" 度人經 , short for the "Yuán Shǐ Wú Liàng Dù Rén Shàng Pǐn Miào Jīng"元始無量度人上品妙經, the "Primal Beginning Boundless Salvation

Highest Level Mystical Scripture", book 5 of the Daoist canon, the first LingBao scripture in the canon.

There are 61 scrolls that comprise the scripture, each following a similar pattern, each with a different focus.

Scrolls 21 to 26 are translated by Norman Goundry on the website http://www.dztranslation.org/

This document is a translation of Scroll 53; it's a story of the five elements, the five colors, the five directions, the five Qi, and the five emperors, translated by charlie5; it's a story of the universe, by the universe, for the universe.

Translation

元始無量度人上品妙經卷之五十三

yuán shǐ wú liàng dù ren shàng pǐn miào jīng juà zhī wǔ shí sān

Primal Beginning Boundless Salvation Highest Level Mystical Scripture - scroll 53

元始無量度人上品妙經卷之五十三

斬滅五行邪怪品

道言昔於玉靈天中明景謠歌大威神土受元始度人斬滅五行邪怪無量上品元始天尊當說是經周迴十過以召十方始當詣座大真大神上聖高尊妙行真人五帝真官明威大將斬邪吏陰陽三五總統官曹紫微神兵無鞅數眾乘空而求金暉映虛寶豐仙感華光羽蓋經轡晨寶萬景交明煥耀八圓七日七夜十方仙真層櫐寶闕洞化相通天綱停個星絡正度神風微肩妙靄凝香氣融和海嶽澄清一國地土山川林木緬千一等無復高下土皆作華玉瑩鮮五明之色眾真侍座元始

Primal Beginning Boundless Salvation Highest Level Mystical Scripture - scroll 53 - Chapter on Chopping off and Extinguishing the Five Elements' Mysterious Evils

The Dao says, in former times, ah! the numinous spirit energy of the jade Heavens, and at its center, the bright scene, singing and dancing the poetry of the road with awe-inspiring power, the spirit of the earth receiving and accepting the primal origin, the salvation that cuts off and extinguishes the mysterious evils drifting through the five elements, the boundless and illimitable, highest level primal origin; the Heavenly venerable undertook to explain with scripture the circuit that revolves circling the ten directions, crossing over past transgression in order to gather all together, summoning everyone in the ten directions to begin to undertake the journey to the throne of truth, the spirit ascending to the holiness of the lofty venerable mysterious conduct of truth, the five emperors' truth officers' effulgent light an inspirational greatness with the will that goes forward chopping away, cracking and splitting the bizarre and harmful demon road of crafty evil, YIN and YANG and "the three and the five" riding together, to lead, govern, command, and unify, officer grade of the purple profound spirit soldiers, with no discontent or dissatisfaction, driven without a yoke and walking without the discomfort of hurry, repeatedly coming in multitudes with their vehicles across the emptiness, their flowing energy arriving as the golden sunshine that radiates its revolving projection through the void, the precious carriage of immortality, the blazing upward whirlwind of soaring elegance, the flowering rays, feathers of the immortal phoenix coiling around the dense growth of passions and delusions below, covering all with the morning's red tinged clouds' radiance, the 10,000 scenes intersecting with bright clarity, the lustrous, brilliant, glorious eight perfect spheres of wholeness (* the eight fundamental characteristics of the school of perfection 1- to teach, 2- Ruling principle, 3-wisdom, 4- to give up or abstain from something, 5- conduct of thought, word, and deed, 6- seat or throne, 7- primary cause which produces effects, and 8- the fruits or results of that primary cause); seven days and seven nights the immortal watches the multistoried tower of truth as it appears in its phases, as the unimpeded universal pervades, and he pauses to delay with Heaven's guide rope, lingering with the stars, connecting to their continuous rectificatory fibers of salvation, concentrating on the wind from the tiny profound fans as it condenses into the dew of fragrant Qi, as if melting out of the harmony onto seas and mountain peaks as they purify into clarity, cool and refreshing in the lonely desert, elegant, serene, and far reaching throughout the one nation of the earth, the dark ground, the mountains, their flowing streams, the forests and trees, all distant and remote, all even in the calm and peace of the one universal 'equal everywhere' class; from the loftiness of the 'never return', below the earth of all and each is regarded as a flower, a lustrous jade, smooth, bright, transparent crystal, with the rare color of the five lights (the five wisdoms) the multitudes gathered together to attend upon the throne of the truth of the primal origin;

五文 wǔ wén

"the five manifest illustrious signs of the elegant, literary culture that enshrines the Dao"

豐 fēng - abundant, rich   寶 bǎo - precious, treasure   咸 xián - all, together, harmonious

通 tōng - pervade, permeate   臺 tái - temple platform

The Heavenly venerable mysterious seat of emptiness floats over the bright scenery, mountains like bells reflecting the auspicious sunshine that blazes and dazzles, the dragon spirit driving the expedition of transformation as it flies on the Royal Road of Heaven like a boat on a long river from the throne of Heaven's origin; explaining the first meaning of the scripture, that the great sages of all the various Heavens gather together in the mountain temple of time and invoke the golden balanced steelyard to weigh the wellness and wholeness below the clouds, praising the good and repairing the evil within time in the one country, men and women abstaining, cutting off, extinguishing the five desires of their passions and affinities (wealth, lust, fame, food, and sleep); explaining the second meaning of the scripture, that the five transformations, the variations among the five elements in their changing development, progress in extended increase, into a plenty that thunders in a deep and thick rumble of flourishing prosperity; explaining the third meaning of the scripture, that the five planets, in their flow like horizontal weaving threads in their weft across the sky, are the five stars to obey, follow, and imitate in their rut, their path of precedence; explaining the fourth meaning of the scripture, that the five Qi (wind, rain, heat, cold, and sunshine) provide for the unceasing calm and tranquility that evens out the myriad things into an eloquent and lofty stillness that dries out and calms down the widespread substance into a smooth and easy prosperity; explaining the fifth meaning of the scripture, that the five eternal virtues (benevolence, righteousness, propriety, wisdom and fidelity) are undisturbed by the greedy beasts, and the world is managed like a flowing river by the Dao, preventing floods and providing stability, illnesses treated, banks rebuilt and repaired, and diseases and pests eliminated, as the river flows and the days progress into the new;   explaining the sixth meaning of the scripture, that the five transports (of the elements and their Qi), the 'five movements' across the five seasons, trundle forward, the wheel pushing forward the platoon, days pushing forward through the chaos, and overthrowing the country of the death road, joining in a harmonized unity to avoid disharmonious irregularity that is contrary to the great ritual, obediently avoiding deviation so as not to let the heart become lost in the sea of transgression; explaining the seventh meaning of the scripture, that the five manifest illustrious signs of the elegant, literary culture that enshrines the Dao spread out to become known, to teach the mysterious crimson and open out the brightness; explaining the eighth meaning of the scripture, that the five divinities of the human spirit (consciousness, thinking, emotional activity, disposition, and spirit), guard, defend, and keep watch utilizing the beautiful majesty of light and wind, to proclaim the widespread imperial edict like a bright torch that opens up the clarity of truth, the Qi overflowing to satisfy and ring the bell tone of fullness in a river chorus that shows the bright clarity, a pool of light and a cleansing wind to wash away the inauspicious evils; explaining the ninth meaning of the scripture, that the five essences of the five internal organs (the heart, lungs, liver, spleen, and kidneys) are reared and nourished to solidify with strength, consolidated to be sturdy and stable, and to be defended like a secret treasure, protected like a baby in swaddling clothes, raised to radiate the bright energy of the spirit world; explaining the tenth meaning of the scripture, that the internal mysterious demons of the five elements are entirely and without exception ruined, lost, the entire road of wild and black clouds gone, they are dispersed from the one country in the temple of time, where of all the men and all the women there are, there is none who does not pour out their heart, emptying it in each and every case, to receive, accept, and endure the protective shelter of salvation, everyone together in harmony to obtain eternal life; The Dao says there is a time before the world, the mysterious, undivided, original beginning, where the Celestial Venerable of the Primordial Beginning explained the scripture's first meaning, showing the solution to the universe - the eastern direction's everlasting, limitless, immeasurable chapter of cracking, splitting, and extinguishing, its pure essence of mountain green water washing away the bizarre and harmful demon road of crafty evil, all the loose and wayward, strange and impractical rocks from that isolated demon road brought to rest in the ocean, arriving at their mysterious, profound, subtle and marvelous truth in the great spirit of divinity, with no discontent or dissatisfaction, driven without a yoke and walking without the discomfort of hurry, as its multitude float empty across the void to achieve perfection; explaining the scripture's second meaning, showing the solution to the universe - the southern direction's everlasting, limitless, immeasurable chapter of cracking, splitting, and extinguishing, its red essence washes away that demon road, the mysterious demons arriving at their mysterious, profound, subtle and marvelous truth in the great spirit of divinity, with no discontent or dissatisfaction, driven without a yoke and walking without the discomfort of hurry, as its multitude float empty across the void to achieve perfection; explaining the scripture's third meaning, showing the solution to the universe - the western direction's....

無極無量品斬滅皓精邪怪至眞大神無鞅之眾浮空而至說
經四遍北方無極無量品斬滅黑精邪怪至眞大神無鞅之眾
浮空而至說經五遍東北無極無量品斬滅火行遊精邪怪至
眞大神無鞅之眾浮空而至說經六遍東南無極無量品斬滅
金行遊精邪怪至眞大神無鞅之眾浮空而至說經七遍西南
無極無量品斬滅水行遊精中央黃精邪怪至眞大神無鞅之
眾浮空而至說經八遍西北無極無量品斬滅木行遊精邪怪
至眞大神無鞅之眾浮空而至說經九遍上方無極無量品斬
滅天元五行邪怪至眞大神無鞅之眾浮空而至說經十遍下
方無極無量品斬滅地元五行邪怪至眞大神無鞅之眾浮空

....everlasting, limitless, immeasurable chapter of cracking, splitting, and extinguishing, its luminous white essence washes away that demon road, the mysterious demons arriving at their mysterious, profound, subtle and marvelous truth in the great spirit of divinity, with no discontent or dissatisfaction, driven without a yoke and walking without the discomfort of hurry, as its multitude float empty across the void to achieve perfection; explaining the scripture's fourth meaning, showing the solution to the universe - the northern direction's everlasting, limitless, immeasurable chapter of cracking, splitting, and extinguishing, its black essence washes away that demon road, the mysterious demons arriving at their mysterious, profound, subtle and marvelous truth in the great spirit of divinity, with no discontent or dissatisfaction, driven without a yoke and walking without the discomfort of hurry, as its multitude float empty across the void to achieve perfection; explaining the scripture's fifth meaning, showing the solution to the universe - the northeastern direction's everlasting, limitless, immeasurable chapter of cracking, splitting, and extinguishing, the fire element rambles and wanders like a flag in a stream, it's pure essence washing away the bizarre and harmful demon road of crafty evil, all the loose and wayward, strange and impractical rocks from that isolated demon road brought to rest in the ocean, arriving at their mysterious, profound, subtle and marvelous truth in the great spirit of divinity, with no discontent or dissatisfaction, driven without a yoke and walking without the discomfort of hurry, as its multitude float empty across the void to achieve perfection; explaining the scripture's sixth meaning, showing the solution to the universe - the southeastern direction's everlasting, limitless, immeasurable chapter of cracking, splitting, and extinguishing, the metal element rambles and wanders like a flag in a stream, it's pure essence washing away the bizarre and harmful demon road of crafty evil, all the loose and wayward, strange and impractical rocks from that isolated demon road brought to rest in the ocean, arriving at their mysterious, profound, subtle and marvelous truth in the great spirit of divinity, with no discontent or dissatisfaction, driven without a yoke and walking without the discomfort of hurry, as its multitude float empty across the void to achieve perfection; explaining the scripture's seventh meaning, showing the solution to the universe - the southwestern direction's everlasting, limitless, immeasurable chapter of cracking, splitting, and extinguishing, the water element rambles and wanders like a flag in a stream, the pure essence of the vast yellow center washing away the bizarre and harmful demon road of crafty evil, all the loose and wayward, strange and impractical rocks from that isolated demon road brought to rest in the ocean, arriving at their mysterious, profound, subtle and marvelous truth in the great spirit of divinity, with no discontent or dissatisfaction, driven without a yoke and walking without the discomfort of hurry, as its multitude float empty across the void to achieve perfection;

explaining the scripture's eighth meaning, showing the solution to the universe - the northwestern direction's everlasting, limitless, immeasurable chapter of cracking, splitting, and extinguishing the wood element rambles and wanders like a flag in a stream, its pure essence washing away the bizarre and harmful demon road of crafty evil, all the loose and wayward, strange and impractical rocks from that isolated demon road brought to rest in the ocean, arriving at their mysterious, profound, subtle and marvelous truth in the great spirit of divinity, with no discontent or dissatisfaction, driven without a yoke and walking without the discomfort of hurry, as its multitude float empty across the void to achieve perfection; explaining the scripture's ninth meaning, showing the solution to the universe - the upper direction's everlasting, limitless, immeasurable chapter of cracking, splitting, and extinguishing, the Heavenly origin of the five elements uses its pure essence to wash away the bizarre and harmful demon road of crafty evil, all the loose and wayward, strange and impractical rocks from that isolated demon road brought to rest in the ocean, arriving at their mysterious, profound, subtle and marvelous truth in the great spirit of divinity, with no discontent or dissatisfaction, driven without a yoke and walking without the discomfort of hurry, as its multitude float empty across the void to achieve perfection; explaining the scripture's tenth meaning, showing the solution to the universe - the upper direction's everlasting, limitless, immeasurable chapter of cracking, splitting, and extinguishing, the earthly origin of the five elements uses its pure essence to wash away the bizarre and harmful demon road of crafty evil, all the loose and wayward, strange and impractical rocks from that isolated demon road brought to rest in the ocean, arriving at their mysterious, profound, subtle and marvelous truth in the great spirit of divinity, with no discontent or dissatisfaction, driven without a yoke and walking without the discomfort of hurry, as its multitude float empty across the void ....

述義聊□
而至十遍周竟十方無極斬滅五行邪怪天真大神一時同至
一國男女傾心歸仰來者有如密雲細霧無鞅之眾連國一半
土皆傾陷非可禁止於是元始化一圓象大小無常煒耀五色
在空玄之中去地九丈元始登引天真大神上聖高尊妙行真
人五帝真官明威大將斬邪騎吏陰陽三五總統官晉十方斬
滅五行邪怪至真神王紫微神兵三天給事無鞅數眾俱入圓
象之中天人仰看惟見拂拂從圓象中入旣入圓象不知所在
國人廓散地還平正無復陷元始卽於圓象之內說經都竟
眾真監度以授於我當此之時毒慶難言法事粗悉諸天復位
俢欻之閒寂無遺響是時天人遭值經法普得濟度全其本年

...to achieve perfection; the ten explanations altogether in the end revolving with the ten directions, everlasting, unbounded, and infinite, chopping away to extinguish the bizarre and harmful demon road of mysterious evil within the five elements, the great spirit of Heaven's truth all at one time arriving at perfection in the one country, men and women overturning and emptying out hearts and minds to return and surrender, looking upward with respect, to arrive at the place that exists hidden behind the clouds, the secret and deep exquisite memorial hall, subtle and wonderful like a mist, as they walk unhurriedly away from the crowd and the cramped, forced pressure and haste of half the country of earth, where the multitude collapse, pouring out their essence and being captured by the pit of fault, falling into the enemy array, submerging and drowning into the victim soup of mistakes; they simply must be able to endure, restraining the self from taboos, standing and bearing the prison court, halting and silencing, putting to rest the active mind and centering steadily in the abstraction; ah!, the primal origin leads transformation magically into salvation with it's single sphere of wholeness, all shapes large and small flickering and glowing with brilliance, their chanting heart shining the light of the five colors that exists at the center of the hollow void, in the clear mind, the still and quiet mysterious emptiness, apart from the space and time of the world's nine feet of rock, ripening in ascent into the primal origin, on the sacrificial journey out of the valley and into the height of mystery, stretching into the truth of the great spirit of divinity, ascending into the holiness of saints, the lofty, venerable, profound and beautiful mystery and wonder that is the truth of the elements, man walking with the five emperors and the officers of truth, walking with the shine of enlightenment in the majestic force of wind and light, accepting the great invitation from the commander-in-chief into the rites of chopping and splitting away from the bizarre magic of the demon road, riding with the spirit officials, YIN and YANG, the three and the five, all gathered in a focused beam that commands and unites to lead the realm of the ten directions, chopping away and extinguishing the crafty evil mysteries from the heart of the five elements, the strange chaos of pathogenic temperament that is the demon road, to arrive at the perfection of profound truth, the subtle marvelous presence of the moral behavior of the saint, unexpectedly flying up to the truth spirit king, and the purple profound wonderful mystery class of spirit soldiers across the three skies, who provide for and serve the affairs below, progressing, content and unhurried, to repeatedly enumerate the multitudes, entirely and without exception, seeing that all equally enter into the sphere of wholeness,

yī yuán

"single sphere of wholeness"

mankind imitating the center of Heaven, looking upward reverently to call on and to depend on Heaven, and to watch out for danger by examining and reflecting from Heaven's perspective, alone in pure dedicated and single-minded thought to see truth, to brush away the dust, whisking it wind blown while following the fullness of the whole, as the center enters into the wonderful understanding that is already round, full, and whole, complete, and perfect, imitating its appearance, with no discriminating thought and pondering on the relative knowledge of place within the nation of men, the big and empty scattered distraction, the loose and separate flowers of the world, but instead returning to the level tranquil calm and peaceful equality of the upright , not repeating the absurd complexity of again and again filling up and emptying the water from the branch while plunging deeper and deeper into the pit, falling deeper and deeper into the trap, but rather stepping out of the chaos and into the primal mysterious origin that is - ah! - like the inside of the round sphere of wholeness; the theory being expounded in the sacred scripture

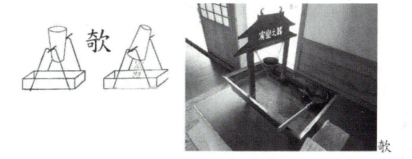

is that in the end, finally all the multitude are inspected by the perfect mirror of truth and unexpectedly at last are directed toward salvation in order to deliver - ah! - the true Self, adequate and able to bear this temple of time with joyful and courteous celebration through all disaster and distress with the words of the teaching, the method and practice through the coarse, thick, wild and rough unpolished surface of phenomena, in all cases learning, comprehending, expounding and utilizing all of the diverse Heavens in order to return to the original state, like river water returning to the sky, with a crashing sound the return to the original place is sudden, Heaven and earth left behind, idle in the distance, silent in the gap, calm and tranquil in nirvana, composed and solitary in the quiet perishable nothingness, if by chance, to suffer and sustain each other unexpectedly, a time with opportunity to create meaningful value along the straight path of the scriptures, following their method for universal salvation, so that all are permitted to cross the stream in unison, to bring about the stone word out of the yellow sand, to ferry the living across the sea of reincarnation to the shore of nirvana, to aid and liberate all, completing the journey of the single root of the entirety across the sea of years;

鈕若中傷傾士歸仰咸行正心不欹不陷不諂不佞不猥不慢
不戾不乖不妬不惡言行平直智識剛明齊慧悟異骨和同
國安民康欣樂冲融經始出教一國以道共有至心崇奉禮敬
皆得度世
道言元始天尊說經中所言並是諸天上帝內名隱韻之音亦
是真魔內諱斬滅五行邪怪百靈之隱名也非世上之常辭上
聖已成真人通玄究微能悉其章誦之十過諸天讚詠五靈敬
侍金木水火元土合并神粹凝和毒害不生混養內化洞冥至
真邪怪鬼祇無綠而與至學之士誦之十過則五帝鑑觀九真
舉仙邪試滅迹怪禍永鎦道業保固善行克全所以爾者通感

道藏輯要　　　　度人妙經　　　壹　　九集四

There is no suffering, wounding, harming, or injury, when all the dust of the earth is overturned and poured out, and people return restored and committed to 'facing upward', everyone's practice of thought, word, and deed dedicated to correctness, with upright heart and mind; none of the absurd complexity of again and again filling up and emptying the water hanging from the branch while plunging deeper and deeper into the pit, no falling into the trap of the enemy's array, no lying or deceit, no eloquent clever and insincere flattery, no vicious dog fighting, no stubborn , willful, obstinate perversity, no absurdly bent, brutal and violent Qi of scourge and disaster, blight and pestilence, no shrewd and clever perversity of the grotesque, the awkward and unreasonable temperament of blocked and separated isolation, no corruption of jealousy and envy, no evil hate, loathing, or wickedness; words and practice all equal, calm, and tranquil on the simple straight and upright path of wisdom, the understanding holding firm, tough as a strong bow, the bright shine of perfect tranquility together with the wisdom of enlightenment that comprehends, the heart of the five aroused through contradiction into a brilliant awareness of mystery in clarity, all the diverse disparities of separation held together in a framework of bone, all held together in a skeleton of blended harmony, the country content and still, safe and secure, the people peaceful, in hale repose, rich with abundance, a harvest of well being extending in all directions, a stable prosperity, delighted in vitality, Heaven and earth singing together the joyful tune of vigorous development, rejoicing together in the red infusion of salvation into truth, everything melting into harmony, fusing and interpenetrating as the bright purple smoke rises like happy music, warm and comfortable, and melting into light; the sacred scripture begins to emerge in order to teach the one country of the world, in order to explain the Dao, like an elephant leading the way in advance of the arrival of the heart that is perfected into mystery, the subtle model and realization of the magic that is bestowed on the reverent hands that hold and accept the divinity, that comply with the divine ceremony with courtesy and etiquette, with reverence and veneration, all and each obtaining the salvation of the world and the epoch together; the Dao says: Yuanshi Tianzun - "Celestial Venerable of the Primordial Beginning" - explains the scripture's central mark, where the words are combined to ascend to all the diverse Heavens and the emperors, with their inner secret sounds of hidden truth; hidden within the beautiful tones are also the true devils, the hundred evil magics with taboo names that are to be chopped, split away, and extinguished, the five elements' bizarre and harmful demon road of crafty evil wayward ghosts and their hidden spirit energy! The blame and reproach of the modern world from the perspective of eternity is contained in these phrases; the ascended holiness of the saints and sages who have already reached perfection into truth permeates man's investigation into the dark mystery; the tiny profound secret has the capability of a bear-like beast, secluded and able to bear bottomless energy in order to investigate the pattern of what grows out from the root, and it is the seal that exposes with a bell-sound, chiming a memorial of the chapter as it recites the song of the ten directions, as they cross over the various kinds of transgression and into Heaven, a chanted song that praises Heaven as the five spirits (Lin, phoenix, tortoise, dragon, and white tiger) venerate and attend upon metal, wood, water, fire, and mysterious dark yellow earth, bringing all together in an accord and unison of poetry that flutters through the mind like prayer in the enveloped dark, a poetry shot from the arrow of the seal, where the pure and elegant divine essence is in harmony, the poison evil of the harm horse of disaster and calamity separated from pure life within the dark chaos, pure life cultivated, reared and nurtured internally, transforming in the cave in darkness and obscurity to arrive at the perfection of profound truth, the demon road with its strange magic ghosts everywhere having no connection, no opportunity, no chance, life only allowed to flourish when it arrives into the marvelous subtle presence of holiness, the learning by the gentleman scholar of the ten directions going past transgression, to the pattern of the five emperors' example in the jade mirror, observed from the Daoist watchtower of nine by immortals of truth who carry up the quiet night thinking, raised heads looking at the moon, harmful demon road of temptation extinguished, blown out like a light, the strange ghosts of disaster and calamity left in ruins beneath the divine blessing of eternal life, driven away by the bright clean industry of the Dao that guards, protects, and defends, and strengthens into solidity, nurturing the good into perfection, the auspicious into holiness, so that virtuous practice is able to overcome, defeat, subdue, and shoulder the whole, in order to permeate and influence the universe.

度亡戰書

五行之神蕩伏邪怪召制威靈克成至道和合眞氣保育人命
得躋立境降會高眞不死而已豈復更生輕誦此章身則被殃
供養尊禮門戶與隆世世昌熾與善因緣萬災不干神明護門
斯經尊妙獨步玉京度人無量爲萬道之宗巍巍大範德難可
勝
道言凡誦是經十過諸天齊到十方斬滅五行邪怪之神剗絕
魔精五行之內不爲殃禍災答承消用保祥而運化常寧安
鎭宰土普承玄恩仁壽高樂清靜自然也上學之士修誦是經
消滌邪害道氣清眞世人受誦則元眞受妙惑念永忘全其壽
年後皆得受鍊度之道毘神暫滅不經地獄卽得返形遊行太

The divine spirit of the five elements is like a pool that cleanses, as it lies low, like a tiger waiting close to the ground to defeat its enemy, the loose rocks of chaos on the demon road, summoning the restraining majestic power of beautiful wind and light to overcome, defeat, capture, forbear, subdue, and pacify the whole so that it arrives into perfection, in the subtle and marvelous presence of the Dao, blending and uniting in harmony like a family of bodies in concord as it enters into the wholeness of the monastery of truth that defends and protects the Qi with the teaching of preservation and righteousness for the destiny of man, allowing the possibility to ascend like a rainbow out of the chaos, into the deep and profound mystery of the sphere's borders, surrendering into the blessing of the lofty assembly, the warm, grand and dignified masterpiece of sweet refreshing richness, the lofty truth of the secluded mountain high above death, the immortality that is joyful and triumphant, crossing beyond death into the victorious recovery of eternal regeneration; simple, easy, and gentle chanting of the elegant patterns, the flag-like embroideries of the music of the chapter, is the sacrifice that covers the life of the body like a quilt, the practice of the body calendar flooded by the wind and rain of grace that saves the people from misfortune and disaster, the sacrificial offering that rears and nourishes with beauty, the venerable ceremony of ritual and prayer that is the gateway portal to rise into grand lofty prosperity that flourishes from age to age in the blazing effulgence, taking part in the virtuous correction of evil, skillfully participating in the auspicious cause that produces effects in another stage of existence, shielded from the ten thousand calamities by the bright divine spirit, and the gateway teaching that guards and protects, defends and shelters, these venerable, mystical scriptures walking alone across the jade capital, bringing immeasurable salvation for the Dao's myriad realizations that rise up lofty and towering above the chaos, the great pattern and model of virtue within difficulty with the force that is able to bear and lift up into the victory of the beautiful scene; the Dao says everyone who chants aloud this scripture into the ten directions celebrates the crossing over of past transgressions, all the diverse Heavens tranquilizing and perfecting, adjusting as they arrive into the ten directions to abandon the confused demons of the spirit of the five elements, drowning the bizarre improprieties as they wash away the demon road, the beauty and light of the ten directions a crusade of suppression that exterminates and annihilates the depravity of wrong into extinction, ending the heart of evil's magic robbery of destiny's vital essence, so the fish of the deep well within the five elements do not suffer the scourge of unprovoked disaster, calamity, and misfortune, and are not punished for their faults and mistakes, allowed to just swim in the eternally flowing brightness of immortality as the evening wind is utilized to disperse disaster, defending the secret treasure, training the world into security and happiness, into the auspicious good fortune that comes from the continuous transport of the revolving Heavenly wheel of perpetual transformation into repose and contentment, and calm, quiet stillness, forged by the weight of the golden truth, the whole face of the earth holding and bearing the obedient inheritance of the red light into open hands that are then pressed together in reverence, accepting the dark profound mystery of grace, the mysterious aura of favor and compassion landing upon the heart, the grace of virtue, rich with the joyful fullness of longevity in the pure and clear stillness that blossoms naturally; ascending to the learning of the gentleman officer's cultivation by chanting this scripture digests and vanishes, cleanses and washes away the harm horse that wanders into instability on the bizarre and harmful demon road of crafty evil, with the Dao's clear, pure, and settled Qi of truth; the people of the worldly epoch who receive, accept, and endure the scripture's meaning, are receiving, accepting, and enduring the pattern of the wonderful, mystical truth, puzzlement of the misleading realm of dark faint confusion and doubt with its passion and temptation forgotten, replaced by enduring mindfulness of the eternally flowing brightness of immortality, the idea of wandering in life and death set aside in the beauty of simply extending years into long life, and later all and each allow the receive-accept-endure of the smelting refinement that trains and governs all into a connected necklace of perfection that is the Dao's salvation, and the divine spirit within that is the wizard flower soul, in its temporary extinguishment, does not proceed into the suffering of the earth prisons, but at once approaches and obtains the golden, empty, leisurely clouds, the body marching in a parade across the great (vast empty clarity);

空此經微妙普度無第一切天人莫不受慶無量之福生死蒙
惠上天所寶不傳下世至十齋金寶效心盟天而傳輕泄漏慢
殃及九祖長役考官侍經五帝玉童玉女各三十六人營衛神
文保護受經者身
道言正月長齋誦詠是經召上元將軍斬滅五行邪怪不正之
祅卽使天界澄廓七燿常明七月長齋誦詠是經召中元官將
斬滅五行邪怪不正之精保佑兆民使安其生十月長齋誦詠
是經召下元君將吏五嶽兵馬斬滅五行邪怪不正之靈安
鎮天下慶祐君親歷世綿長後天而存八節之日誦詠是經召
天地四方八極兵馬御絕魔靈順布五氣長養生成本命之日

...vast empty clarity; the scripture turns with the warp that goes through the sky full of tiny exquisite secret wonders, the torrent of boundless universal salvation, and in the whole of Heaven there is none who does not receive, accept, and endure its heart of joy, and the blessed immeasurable treasure of happiness and longevity, life and death covered over by the grace of the fresh water of the benevolent heart of Heaven that enables life to ascend into the Heavenly jewel, unencumbered by the world below, to reach the mysterious profound truth that the gentleman officer receives into both hands to nurture in righteousness, within the precious gold and jade shell that brings his heart into alliance with Heaven, while the typical and reckless leakage and loss of mistake, the impure flow of the mind, the taints of the stream of transmigration, the pride, arrogance and laziness that invite damage, disaster, and death into the pool, are avoided, in conjunction with sunlight, water, and air, and with the nine ancestors, the founders and patriarchs, in eternal service, guarding the frontier, testing longevity with the years, priestly officials attending upon the sacred book of the five emperors, the jade boy and jade girl, and the thirty six battalions guarding and protecting health so that the straight line does not sink into the night, the divine spiritual writing guarding the secret treasure, preserving the body, blessing and protecting righteousness with its armor seal, the inner and outer self sheltered by receiving, accepting, and enduring the scriptures with one's body and one's life, absorbing the river of sacrifice into personal experience in order to be the bones of the world; the Dao says on the correct months always fasting in purification, singing the eternal sound, the chanting and chanting of these scriptures, invites the upper mysterious origin to send its military, to chop away and put to rest the harmful ghosts, the anomalies of incorrectness and iniquity within the five elements, the bewitching enchantments that are the passions and afflictions, all the distress and vexations of worldly cares, and purifying the self into the clarity that opens out into the expansive silence of Heaven's borders, where the seven radiances are perpetually bright and clear; on the seventh month always fasting to purify and singing the music of the scriptures calls together the center of the mysterious essential undivided origin, and its high priest official will chop apart and wash away the bizarre and harmful demon road of injustice within the five elements, their vital essence defended by the righteous armor, the palace guarded by garrisons with the omen, the people made to be calm, still, quiet and safe, secure in their pure life; on the tenth month always fasting to purify and chanting the flying scriptures summons the lower mysterious origin's official monarch who will send his public officials of the five sacred peaks, with their soldiers on horseback preparing the road with their omen that handles anything, flowing through the chaos with sacrifice that washes away the defilement of the five elements' mysterious evil ghosts of impropriety, their spiritual power annihilated, the deep well of the five elements restored to peace and contentment, their safe harbor guarded by weight the surrounding golden truth, the divine grace of Heaven's joyful blessing flowing from beyond human understanding into the open and attentive hands, and the monarch gentleman ruler blessing parents and close ancestors to pass vivid and clear through the calendar of their lifetimes like soft continuous floss through eternity, to anterior Heaven, (early Heaven, 'before' Heaven, from before earth was separated from Heaven), and to rest and be preserved there; on the eight festival days, singing and chanting these scriptures invites "the Heaven and Earth quartet octupole array", the "far-off all directions" military forces on horseback, flowing inward downstream through the gaps to break off and end the flow of the Qi of the devil's realm, in a wonderful conquest by the spirit power that howls in the wind and rain through the thatched windows and in the dance of the shaman, as the evil ways of the demons vanish into nothingness, following along with the outspreading declaration of the five Qi in its constant rearing, nourishment, and support of pure life in the journey of becoming into perfection; on birthdays - ('root foundation of life's destiny' days)......

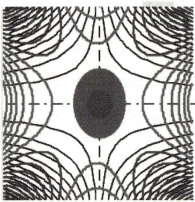

天地四方八極
tiān dì sì fāng bā jí

"the Heaven and Earth quartet octupole array", the "far-off all directions"

道藏輯要

誦詠是經名天元九宮星宿真官威殺之神檢校命籙五行邪
怪祛斬滅蹤五神守正萬氣資形生道靈堅超還上清
道言行道之日皆當香湯沐浴齋戒入室東向叩齒三十二
通上聞三十二天心拜三十二過閉目靜思身坐青寅三
色雲氣之中內外翕冥有青龍白虎朱雀玄武獅子白鶴羅
列左右日月照明洞煥室內萬生圓象光映十方如此分明
密咒曰
无上玄元大上道君召出臣身中三五功曹左右官使者侍香
玉童傳言玉女五帝直符直日香官各三十二人關啟所言今
日吉慶長齋滿堂修行至經無量度人願所啟上徹徑御

无上三十二天元始上帝至尊几前畢
引炁三十二過東向誦經

....singing and chanting the eternal sound of the scriptures calls on Heaven's origin, in nine-temple-palace, the night lodge of the constellations, so that the officers of truth, with the majestic power and authority of the wind and light, will examine and restrain the divine spirits of ending life, proofreading the jade record prophecy, the mysterious instrument of life's destiny, the character map made of Qi, decoupling disaster, using wind to dispel calamity and ward off evil, removing dust and expelling the netherworldly chaos of the demon road, all traces of its curses washed away, the five divinities of the heart, gods of the life and the spirit of the mind - (the human spirit, consciousness, thinking, emotional activity, and disposition) - guarding and defending correctness, the myriad resources of the Qi provided to the body, the pure life of the Dao's spirit energy providing the strength and solidity to pass over into transcendence, moving in an ascending spiral, clean and indifferent, away from the residue of earth, into pure and transparent clarity, like a cool, midnight breeze; The Dao says, daily practice of the Dao should be fragrant like incense, with an immersive bathing and an undertaking of fasting as a guarding discipline at the entry into home of perfection, facing toward the east, knocking the teeth together 32 times, directed upward to permeate the 32 Heavens, the heart and mind saluting to pass over human transgression and error, holding the eyes closed, and ceasing the thought and attention, into a calm and quiet stillness; with the body sitting among the green, yellow, and red, the three colors of the clouds at the center of the Qi, inside and outside a vigorous, dense, and auspicious mystical obscurity, with the green dragon, white tiger, red sparrow, black warrior, lion and crane, arranged like torches at the doors within the net, and at the left and right, sun and moon, brightly illuminating the cavern that is the brilliant indoor room, where the project of pure life is embraced by the surrounding whole that it imitates as it reflects the bright illuminating shine from the center of the ten directions, the separate branches following along in the shared duties of the effulgence;

the teaching of the secret, is the speech of the clouds;

at the nothing-higher profound mysterious origin, the greatest high monarch of the Dao summons everyone with an invitation to emerge into the beyond, with eyes of immortality stretched open like the bow of an aimed arrow, the body centered in the three and the five, with meritorious ministers and governing officials to the left and the right employed to instruct and to serve, sweet smelling incense measuring the time as the jade boy speaks the words, like a mysterious cloud suddenly transferred to paper and passed on to the jade girl, the five emperors' unexpectedly direct and simple narrative solution, honest words of straightforward, blunt, verbal integrity, teaching the value of the months, of duty, of the movement of rotation, with meaning encrypted in the straight chops beside the hidden bend, upright and victorious discipline leading one to be a direct link in a mountain chain, words arranged into a talisman that shines direct like the sun, the fragrant officers, each of the 32 men of the closed off barrier, opening out like the emergence of Venus in the morning sky, with their speech. The present day's auspicious fortune is a celebration growing in length into forever, with a fasting of mind, body, and spirit, into clarity, in the temple hall for the cultivation of virtue, the self-cultivation of practice and learning that leads to the most mysterious and profound truth of boundless universal salvation, pursuing with resolve the opening up and beginning of the enlightenment of the world, and ascending into the thoroughly pervading education into destiny, the royal expedition on the narrow track, the vertical path that resists the enemy Qi, the floating long river rule of imperial policy. The nothing-higher 32 Heavens of Primal Beginning God "Shangdi", most mysterious and perfect venerable at the marvelous sacrificial altar spirit seat, is the guide for the future, stretching and guiding to lead the magical Qi of the 32 Heavens as they cross over above, the celebration that transcends all transgression, facing the east and singing the song of the scripture.

Primal Beginning Boundless Salvation Highest Level Mystical Scripture -

The primal beginning is the mystery in the cavern, and the numinous energy in the wind and the rain that is the precious treasure, the "LingBao", is the root, the origin and source; this chapter of the highest grade mystery is about the chief that chops away evil and extinguishes the mysterious demons in the ten directions, revolving in his rotations to ferry mankind to the shore of salvation, past the hundred devils that are hiding in their secret shelters, using the beautiful sound of the tidings to abandon the netherworld and bring the universe together in accord, in a simmering correctness of self-existence occurring naturally and spontaneously with the five Qi (wind rain heat cold and sunlight), the true language within the mystery of emptiness that ascends to divinity from the great muddy torrent; its numinous spirit energy flows from the mouth of the spring out into Heaven, into earth, and into the netherworld; it is the taproot of the unified whole that revolves and transports the five Qi, the origin of the five elements (water fire earth wood and metal), the source of the great transformation that constantly drives everything, the commanding imperial chariot that is difficult to describe, throughout all time it is the continuous and uninterrupted threading of the five elements into the cloth that spreads out and lines up to rear and nourish, to educate physically, mentally, and spiritually, the protective blessing that trains the phenomena of the world, preserving and guiding pure life into the completion of perfection, so that the mistakes of the incorrect path are not made manifest, the incorrect path does not shine, the incorrect path is not set up and established, the incorrect path does not become truth; the complex interlocking mistakes of wrongdoing that plate themselves in gold, in a fog of disharmony and poisonous confusion, omen of epidemic and disaster, bound knots in the misty haze of mysteriously pervasive sources of harm and confusion, are broken up and dispersed, floating away and burning off in the natural self-effulgent light of divine virtue, driven away by the powerful wind of sacrifice: evil warded off, confusion dispelled, disaster decoupled, practice cured, wisdom repaired, and all calamity continuously cut down without stopping, bringing into existence the mysterious and wonderful pattern, the marvelous effect of the teaching of mysterious ascension into the "supreme ultimate", the Tai Ji, the undifferentiated absolute, the oneness before duality that is the primitive order of the universe; the jade barrier and the golden watchtower of the spirit city hold YIN and YANG in their original balance, with the three Qi; it is their pivot point, their center of power, the rotating opening from which they emanate as they extend into the expansive vastness, the grand Qi ocean of the universe; the Qi at first is in perfect harmony and unity, at first freshly cut from the natural green beauty of the jade temple palace, as the revolving illumination of its mystic shine begins to light the front courtyard, the wall and the terrace collecting the clouds, the beautiful natural handover of harmony in the radiant crystal as the secret unbreakable great circuit surrounds the boundary of the ten directions, winding the net around everywhere with green silk thread; at the center there is a blending into melody, the five elements revolving to follow the transformation of the divine spirit; at the center is a flow controlled and managed by an imperial system that is in command and carries the load, the dark mystery of the limits of pure life reared and nurtured by its prince monarch ruler; at the center is an informing tally of the bewitching demons who are exposed, defeated and destroyed, released as their cities are cracked like stone, their "harm horses" of instability and calamity broken and turned to flowers by the great spirit; at the center there is the numinous power of the immortals, written into the jade book of talismans of the imperial elder gentleman of divinity;

at the center there is YIN and YANG, the three treasures, the five Qi, the seven stars and the nine fields of brightness and their rectifying power, composing with a fixed and determined unity the destiny of pure life, the venerable divinity that cuts off and extinguishes the mysterious demons, boundless and inexhaustible ...

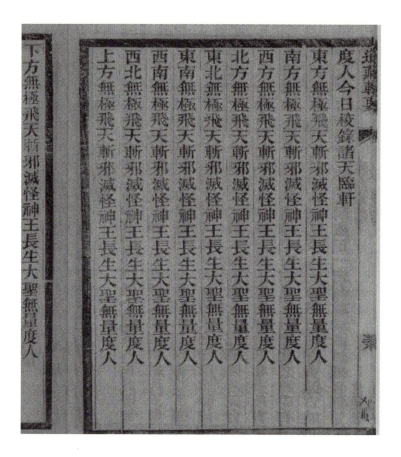

...boundless salvation for the modern day to be studied in the records of the various Heavens overlooking the high pavilion.

From the eastern direction, flying up to Heaven, chopping away the unhealthy influences and extinguishing the mysterious evils, the Spirit King of eternal life is the great sage of boundless salvation;

From the southern direction, flying up to Heaven, chopping away the unhealthy influences and extinguishing the mysterious evils, the Spirit King of eternal life is the great sage of boundless salvation;

From the northern direction, flying up to Heaven, chopping away the unhealthy influences and extinguishing the mysterious evils, the Spirit King of eternal life is the great sage of boundless salvation;

From the western direction, flying up to Heaven, chopping away the unhealthy influences and extinguishing the mysterious evils, the Spirit King of eternal life is the great sage of boundless salvation;

From the north eastern direction, flying up to Heaven, chopping away the unhealthy influences and extinguishing the mysterious evils, the Spirit King of eternal life is the great sage of boundless salvation;

From the south eastern direction, flying up to Heaven, chopping away the unhealthy influences and extinguishing the mysterious evils, the Spirit King of eternal life is the great sage of boundless salvation;

From the south western direction, flying up to Heaven, chopping away the unhealthy influences and extinguishing the mysterious evils, the Spirit King of eternal life is the great sage of boundless salvation;

From the north western direction above, flying up to Heaven, chopping away the unhealthy influences and extinguishing the mysterious evils, the Spirit King of eternal life is the great sage of boundless salvation;

...From the direction below, flying up to Heaven, chopping away the unhealthy influences and extinguishing the mysterious evils, the Spirit King of eternal life is the great sage of boundless salvation;

下方無極飛天斬邪滅怪神王長生大聖無量度人
十方至真飛天斬滅邪怪神王長生度世無量大神並乘晨霞
寶興仙威華光羽蓋驂衛三元官將十極仙靈建斬邪之節滅
怪神旌前嘯洞真之曲後詠靈虛妙歌紫鸞玄鶴吟嘯相和天
逕敵逆龍驤虎翼輾億乘萬騎浮空而來傾光迴監貢度生天
關內宰火鈴上曹監察大魔威禁玄靈紫清主錄監度大神執
麾仗鈇大布威靈齊奉帝符檢錄五行察制萬類造化靈司山
河海嶽經緯星臆八渡九壘十二宮辰祛湯祅武乖沴之慾束
縛惡精邪怪之形不得恣縱逸肆魔孽元始告命勅使神兵斬
邪無鑰開化生津保安正道迴度劫輪真機變鍊妙氣救榮人

度人妙經

...From the direction below, flying up to Heaven, chopping away the unhealthy influences and extinguishing the mysterious evils, the Spirit King of eternal life is the great sage of boundless salvation;

From out of the ten directions, unexpectedly the wooden bird is made to fly toward perfection, toward the most mysterious Dao of profound truth, flying into Heaven, chopping away what is dirty, extinguishing the confusion that leads to error, as the Spirit King grows and develops life into the eternal, ferrying the world across the vast, deep ocean of the relative and into salvation, the great spirit world that is without limitation, and joining with the vehicle of the red-tinged clouds at dawn, merging into the brilliant rosy glow of daybreak, wearing the red radiant luster of the precious clouds, riding the chariot of immortals into the fiery whirlwind of blossoming brightness, covered in feathery plumes and a canopy of speech that protects the mind like the outer two horses of a four horse team, an officer defending the three origins (Heaven's, earth's, and man's), a military commander with the will and the wisdom to lead the ten directions to the pinnacle of immortality, with the spiritual power to save life by breaking up the trains of delusion, blowing out and extinguishing the inner heat of anger and pain with the howling numinous wind, with long streaming spirit pennant flags in front that reverently whistle song in the cavern of truth, and behind them a chant full of spirit energy in the emptiness,

a beautiful and mystical song like a dark red phoenix rising into the spirit realm, toward the mysterious swan that floats beyond Heaven and Earth, a song that that swims in the mighty torrent to the target, the highest mystery and final goal, a proud Heavenward chant that is the appearance of the harmony of Heaven, blending into Heaven to encounter the opening into enlightenment, opening the door with signal fire to flourish and strengthen on the lush and narrow road, with the dragon on the left and the tiger on the right as wings,

and the hundred thousand words as the shafts that connect the myriad horses to the chariot that drifts across the surface of emptiness, arriving with the bright rays that revolve, that harness and pilot the sailing chariot, the jade mirror that inspects the school, the strong and firm supervisor that brings life into the truth of Heaven's salvation, the inside closed off, shut by a barrier in a festival of sacrifice to govern the world, the latch of the door sealed by the flame that ascends into the company of firm rulers, the jade sphere that shakes the golden prison to purify into clarity with the king's stone chisel, the golden reflecting prison set free

(gold and jade axle of pure life)

into Heaven's salvation by the spirit that seizes and takes hold with a rejoicing revolving wave of signal flag banner that turns everything around, the battle Qi of virtue, the weapon that rings like a bell in Heaven, its power spreading outward like a cloth of spirit energy, a starry announcement of vision lined up across the dark road like troops, equalizing and evening out the darkness like a flood that tranquilizes all with fullness, to be received and held in respectful hands, accepting the magic bestowed by the emperor, enshrined in the command to bear thriving fortune, the talisman of restraint and control, the inspection seal carved by the emperor's stone chisel into the five elements carefully inspecting the field with profound observation, the ten thousand kinds of beings simmering in regulation and restraint that prepares and builds into magic with the world's calendar, formulating the precepts that achieve the mysterious realm, the wonderful position of exquisite transformation, with the spiritual energy capable of managing mountains, rivers, and oceans -the spiritual energy imparted by the lofty peaks of the Zodiac of constellations, the course of the Heavenly Bodies in their warp and their weft across the sky, the orbital rotating dance that is all practice and path, the rituals of the eight seas of the world, the nine fields of Heaven, and the twelve palaces of the constellations forever sacrificing to drive away the burning acidic hot springs of calamity and disaster, to scatter away and dispel the exceedingly evil dust of confusion,

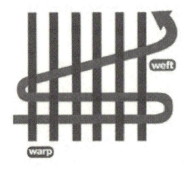

經緯 jīng wěi

to ascend above the miasma of fault and transgression, to ride above the evil of trespass and negligence, using control and restraint, to bundle and tie afflictions and passions, desire and resentment, hate and shame, fear and slander, to save the essence from the mysterious unhealthy influences; their bewildering forms must not be neglected idly out of laziness and fatigue, not to swim in laziness with idle capacity, not to give free reign and let indulgence and excess rise up, unrestrained, on wanton rampage, extravagant, with luxury and disease presumptuously stretched out and on display, like flocks of devils; the primordial addresses life and fate by shackling and binding with iron restraint, with imperial commands of warnings, Daoist magic that employs a spirit army to decapitate devils and turn them to nothing,

勅 chì - imperial decree; Taoist magic;

so that the magic of transformation can open out into salvation, pure life ferried across the river so that it can reach its destination, defending the precious barrier with armor like swaddling clothes, peace, tranquility, and contentment safe and secure in an upright and correct Dao that revolves with the moon and stars, ferrying mortal life, the wheel that seizes and steals from calamity as it rotates, the wheel of the five elements with truth as its pivot as it transforms in clouds, the chain of smelting refinement, beautiful, mystical, and profound, beyond thought, as the Qi diffuses like powder, a dusting, a dressing on the flower, depositing the YANG as it unfolds the light that shines and teaches, with glory flourishing in clouds and falling gently onto the world of human beings....

十二宮
Twelve Palaces

浮

...no disease can attack, no sharp or violent flashes of terror can slander the day, unexpected or unreasonably harsh, no plague or pestilence of argument, slander, envy or jealousy, can spread, when the spirit of virtue is united in accord with the brightness of effulgence that flows through eternity like a waterfall of salvation, the world no longer trapped with knots of misfortune or stranded in disaster, but equal with Heaven as it moves forward through the years in wholeness, traveling beyond in the chariot of transcendence as the three roads* vanish behind the wall of the wonderful secret, crossing the stream and leaving behind the chaotic flow of suffering, hardship, and bitterness, climbing over and stepping beyond disaster, distress, and adversity, ascending in peace past the devils, to ramble playfully in Heaven's "mysterious-mysterious", luxuriantly prolonging and extending the years stretching long and unbroken in the vastness, a prosperity without color or outward appearance, its region the sphere of Brahman's element.

the "mysterious mysterious"

"the square room, the desolate wasteland"

Eastern Eight Heavens

"Jade gift of bright salvation" Heaven; Emperor "Overlooking the square room, the desolate wasteland, with the topic of refreshment, revival, and rebirth"

"Mysterious silence of solitary and indifferent mind pervades correctness" Heaven; Emperor "Lonely universe silent and empty, floating away to the distant beginning"

"The assisting understanding guards and protects YANG" Heaven; Emperor "Refining the cinnabar with the mysterious music of insight and contemplation"

"Initial wisdom of light revolves on the wheel that cultivates" Heaven; Emperor "the discourse on fullness is the seed that permeates the universe"

"The brilliant spirit pond varies in accord with the transformation of salvation" Heaven; Emperor "Ocean of the rays in the vermilion cavern"

"The square cavern of the inexpressible imperial dimension, quiet, leisurely, and idle, shining with destiny" Heaven; Emperor "Endless and inexhaustible jumping past the disaster and calamity of the harm horse/black sheep"

"The square barn laying the foundation is the fundamental root for the dazzling shine of the illuminating ray" Heaven; Emperor "surging waves upon the universal platform terrace"

"the purple 'lin' - the Chinese female unicorn - summons to immortality" Heaven; Emperor "blessing, happiness, good fortune, living forever"

 lín / The lin, or female unicorn. ancient legend of an animal, like a deer, the body has scales, a tail. Its ancient symbol of good fortune, is also used as a metaphor prominent figures. large female deer, Kirin [kylin; [Chinese] unicorn] (metaphor rare and precious thing) [bright] Lin looks bright with phosphorescence

紫麟召仙天　　　　帝祖長生

南方八天

太妙警晨天　　帝寶策紫微
頂光腹真天　　帝道極祕呈
存玄慶智天　　帝頓希谷仁
傳整滅魔天　　帝駢郱蕩魔
顯生變身天　　帝陰穴露埏
赤寶垂安天　　帝益鹿杏機
錫廣祐明天　　帝堯裴沙庸
洞光敝玄天　　帝何童慇聰

Southern Eight Heavens

"greatest mysterious subtlety of luxuriant daybreak" Heaven; Emperor "precious plan of purple subtlety"

"from the top the bright ray strides across truth" Heaven; Emperor "at the highest point of the Dao the secret memorial petition is revealed"

"Storing up and preserving dark mystery, celebrating wisdom" Heaven; Emperor "suddenly pausing to admire the mountain valley stream of kindness and virtue, primeval river of life"

"teaching the spiritual energy to extinguish devil magic" Heaven; Emperor "the parallel country washes away devils"

"the divine and mysterious transformation of body, mind, and spirit reveals pure life" Heaven; Emperor "scattered and superfluous YIN that was hidden in the shadows is exposed and struck"

"the precious red jewel comes down into peace and tranquility" Heaven; Emperor "the immense benefit of prosperous longevity overflows like sacred deer coming from the quiet and obscure dark mystery's root principle"

"bestowing the reward of happiness and good fortune, the warm glimmering blessing of divinity's bright wisdom" Heaven; Emperor "injustice wearing an ordinary grass coat"

"the ray of reverence and respectful caution in the darkness of obscure mystery penetrating throughout the cavern" Heaven; Emperor "how an innocent child communicates the inexpressible bright intelligence"

西方八天
神文示宗天　帝玉褰上元
虎褰世摽天　帝梵無延康
遊真虛用天　帝謁昌葦龍
正氣符剛天　帝遜香規
測神問封天　帝宣幽述真
奏功證道天　帝運常明
烈地蒼冥天　帝號希淵途
誅怪攝政天　帝處彥邪靈

北方八天

The Western Eight Heavens

"the writings of divine spirit reveal and proclaim the purpose, the model, and the realization" Heaven; Emperor "jade chess pieces ascending to the primal origin"

"a tiger robe the signal banner of the temporary world" Heaven; Emperor "the mystical Brahman does not delay the rich flood of abundance and well-being on the wide road"

"rambling and wandering freely in the truth, employing emptiness" Heaven; Emperor "visiting the flourishing prosperity of light and life, the flower of the dragon" Heaven

"the rectifying Qi of the talisman is benevolent and strong" Heaven; Emperor "looking out into the lofty remote distance at the regulating plan that educates and nurtures life"

"surveying and estimating divine spirit is asking to be bestowed with the imperial seal" Heaven; Emperor "proclamation to the netherworld narrates and explains truth"

"playing the music of meritorious achievement demonstrates the Dao" Heaven; Emperor "the revolving wheel of perpetual effulgence"

"blazing beauty, fresh and brilliant, earth's luxuriant vegetation flourishes over the invisible obscurity of the netherworld" Heaven; Emperor "a bugle call roars with the song of the way, marking the road, full of hope and expectation over the deep black water of the profound abyss"

"executing the mysterious demons of untamed desires, the communicating melody permeates the realm" Heaven; Emperor "the entry point and dwelling place for the elegant and accomplished spirits"

禁鑌百無利元天　帝璛蘌仙
高宸泰微扑崇天　帝鳳華飛綱
洞志幽虛禮剛天　帝文何德揚
九迴轉德恩本天　帝陶邈清
晦俱息康存一天　帝陽文子持
北清總司天　　　帝判皇極峒
玄微察命天　　　帝壽蒙瓮成
鑒神拔獄訊靈天　帝望歐夷卿

三十二天三十二帝諸天隱諱諸天隱名天中空洞自然靈章
諸天隱韻五行之音五行之尊五行之神五行大魔五行之靈

The Northern Eight Heavens

"durable restraint, forbidding taboo and prohibiting harm, stands guard with the weight of the golden balanced steelyard, preventing the hundred unfavorable origins" Heaven; Emperor "the exquisite jade spreads out to cover the immortals"

"the lofty and eminent deep house keeps safe and peaceful the tiny and profound as it dances with purpose, model of the ancestors" Heaven; Emperor "the blossoming phoenix flies up out of the net"

"ambitious resolve in the empty cavern over the netherworld performs the ritual ceremony of rigid strength, firm justice and brave benevolence" Heaven; Emperor "writings on how moral virtue is raised up and propagated"

"the nine fields of Heaven revolve, transforming virtue at the root of thought" Heaven; Emperor "the steep bank of quiet clarity in the profound remote distance"

"the wild trail goes all black, like a spring night rain, resting to breathe, pausing and ceasing, to deposit, store up, preserve, and maintain the one" Heaven; Emperor "YANG writing is the seed to be grasped, maintained, preserved"

"in the north quiet clarity is gathered and assembled to take charge" Heaven; Emperor "discerning judgment of the brilliantly shining imperial ruler in the extreme high-mountain cavern"

"dark mysterious profound subtlety investigates and examines fate" Heaven; Emperor "longevity received from above to provide for accomplishment of perfection"

"the bright spirit mirror patrols the netherworlds to interrogate their spiritual energy" Heaven; Emperor "gazing past the dust, homeward into the full moon distance, wide awake with mystery-probing solitude, taut as a bow, the noble high officer razes and exterminates, weeding out ruin, leaving behind only plain peaceful contentment"

The "32 Heavens and the 32 Emperors" conceals all the diverse Heavens to avoid mentioning the taboo names of all the diverse Heavens, hiding their esoteric names; at Heaven's center is the empty cavern of the "self so", the spontaneous, self-existent spirit energy of Brahman, the chapter of all the diverse Heavens' secret beautiful sounds, the five elements' tidings, the five elements' honor, the five elements' expression of divinity, the five elements' great devils, and the five elements' spirit world;

九和十合變化上清無量玄奧深不可詳數落神真普度天人
今日欣慶受度歷關諸天請滅怪惡斬絕邪源調運五行功參
大元真王鎮御道氣開宣東極化木西極生金北極凝液南極
激炎中極上宮合會四支青帝徽生白帝欽德赤帝盪祇黑帝
收毒黃帝中主萬禍俱息木行大魔飛光寶龍火行大魔燿天
紫童金行大魔返神會容水行大魔駕氣乘風土行大魔劫霞
洞窈五行大魔萬神之宗部率神官出入幽冥橫戈擁甲萬騎
雲奔統攝威伐與道同倫玉天開化察錄神軒靈明通泰蜀祁
無前玉樞擲烈銳八延三將馳騁四帥揚旗擾天觸爛擊雷
散烟敢有干試拒過上真金鉞前戮已天後刑掃除邪怪鳳火

...the nine fields of Heaven mix and blend in harmony with the ten directions, like a united army, like a dancing fire of bright shining divine positive transformation rising into perfect clarity, like thin clear waves running fast and cool through a green forest, lofty, elegant, serene and far reaching, measureless in the deep rich mysterious profound obscurity, unfathomable, ...the nine fields of Heaven mix and blend in harmony with the ten directions, like a united army, like a dancing fire of bright shining divine positive transformation rising into perfect clarity, like thin clear waves running fast and cool through a green forest, lofty, elegant, serene and far reaching, measureless in the deep rich mysterious profound obscurity, unfathomable, spreading out everywhere the blossoming teaching light that descends and falls like leaves of divine spirit, the true reality of Heaven, for mankind, the modern day a joyful celebration of receiving, accepting, and enduring Heaven's salvation. The various Heavens, difficult to express with words and shut behind the barrier, are invited to extinguish the mysterious evils like wind blowing out a match, cutting off the flow of the chaotic stream so that it vanishes into the wonderful surrounding beauty, the origin and spring of transgression investigated, regulated, and reconciled into harmony and melody in the revolving wheel of the five elements, by the power of merit, through meditation and reflection shining like a constellation of stars into the great origin of truth, of the king who guards and defends with the weight of Heaven to manage the Dao's Qi as it unfolds its proclamation; at the Eastern zenith, transformation of the element 'wood', at the western zenith pure life of the element 'metal', at the northern zenith the gathering condensation of the element 'water', at the southern zenith the stimulating rising of the element 'fire", the center's zenith, the upper palace uniting the assembly of the four mysteries; the green emperor guards green, innocent, pure life; the white emperor restrains desire and gives moral virtue; the red emperor sweeps away the enchantment of evil, the black emperor recalls and collects poisons accumulated from the world, and the yellow emperor of the center rules over the myriad disasters, putting an end to all of them together equally; the wood element's great demon - flying bright ray precious dragon; the fire element's great demon - dazzling Heaven of purple youth; the metal element's great demon - divine spirits assemble and gather, returning restored to be held and contained; the water element's great demon - harnessing the Qi to the chariot as it rides on the wind; the earth element's great demon -seizing the red tinged clouds to penetrate the vast dome of the Heavens; the five elements' great demons follow after the myriad sprits' models of realization, their troops commanded by spirit officials that go out and enter in from beyond, evolving knowledge and bringing truth to the understanding in the profound secret invisible darkness; a crosswise spear is held in the armor of the ten thousand mounted soldiers as they gallop across the clouds like a streaming rapids to gather and unify, taking command with power and majesty in a military crusade that takes part in the Dao together with humanity in the Jade of Heaven, unfolding the transformation of salvation, inspecting and recording words and deeds, wicked villain spirits pulled up by the power of the numinous wind and brightness that permeates thoroughly, bringing peace and stability, transforming the turbid and runny into the bright and clear, driving discord from the gaps, cleansing illness from the cavities, nothing left in front of the Jade pivot, the palace of Heaven, floating and spreading in heroic columns, stern and strong to ardently cast lakes of golden joy onto lakes of golden joy; with the music of the eight mysterious sounds driving across the three borders, the four dazzling commanders flying long streamers that touch the brilliant burning flames of Heaven, drumming idealists striking with thunder to scatter the dust and blow away the smoke, leisurely dispelling the soot from the smoke wells of war, so that the dryness of transgression that had dared to exist is examined , tested, and denied, the great offense warded off by hand, the inner city defended, barricades not crossed by the outside world, stopped by the upper true reality, with the golden battle axe out front to eloquently eradicate, and the giant sky of Heaven behind it holding the sacrificial penalty that punishes evil, sweeping away to eliminate the mysterious demons with wind and fire....

```
誰停千千截首萬萬剪形魔無千犯鬼無祇精三官北鄭明檢
鬼營不得容隱金馬驛呈普告無窮萬神咸聽三界五帝列言
上清
玄元妙紀五氣開皇眇眇大混混化微茫上施神華下布靈光
緹緼元梵羅絡乾坤剛柔相感序列五行五行相運造育生成
推蕩無滯和合歸真妙道彌綸運度自然五真流演升降迴旋
施養生化嫣氣如泉五用順常萬類滋繁勝氣傍凌兼位而遷
淫則為癘邪怪起源出為崇祆民物銜冤上帝勅斬敷落五篇
赤書玉字八威龍文保制劫運使天長存梵氣彌羅萬範開張
元綱流演三十二天輪轉無色周迴十方旋斗歷箕回度五行
```

...that does not stop, their great variety intercepted and absolutely cut down by the roaring chief who chases and totally annihilates the devil's magic forms, no dry transgression recurring to offend, no ghosts or demons stealing the pure essence of spirit, the subtle vitality, the quintessence of living beings; the three officials (of the departments of earth, Heaven, and water) at the northern capital brightly inspect the netherworld, to check, and restrain the clever ghosts, their encampment exposed and not tolerated, as the post station of peaceful existence for the golden horses is universally declared to be inexhaustible, endless, and boundless, the spirits in widespread harmony as they listen at the three boundaries (of past, present and future), the five emperors of the five elements lining up and arranging the words to ascend into purity and clarity. At the mysterious origin, the mystic wonderful and profound era, the five Qi open out the royal brilliant light to stare off into the distance at the great turbulent flow of the chaotic darkness, to transform the profound vast boundless confusion, raising it up into a divine spiritual flower, spreading out the cloth of divine energy of spirit onto life with illuminating rays that wrap and coil around like silk floss from the mystical Brahman origin, creating a net of continuous fibers to hold YIN and YANG / sun and moon / Heaven and earth, strong and pliant, with mutual reciprocation of response arranging the five elements; the five elements mutually resonate as they revolve in the rotating net, to form, bring up, and create the world, the mysterious realm reaching the wonderful position at the highest point, rearing and nurturing pure life into perfect completion, investigating without delay, energetically sweeping away and cleansing, and returning the unity and harmony of the true beautiful mysterious wholeness of the Dao that shoots out to reach everywhere as the green silk twists on the revolving wheel of salvation spontaneously and naturally; the true five flow and spread out, performing their play in long streams that circle the world, an underground play that stretches out, far reaching, a sermon with speech winding in unbroken appearance, spread overflowing, miles fluidized in a chant that ascends, a dragon and tiger blessing into tame surrender that curves, revolves, and returns, whirling with the moon and stars, a fluttering flag whose wave bestows the seal, the wind of grace that paints the scenery, nourishing and rearing pure life as that life is transformed through its intimate and peaceful interaction with the Qi, the out flowing spring of the five elements employed to constantly train and manage the energy of the myriad categories as they increase and multiply, permeated with the nourishing tonic, flourishing and prosperous in the lush growth of mystery, victorious as they propagate on the complex and unfamiliar track, their practice guided by the Qi to approach the interlocked doors to immortality, managing the wind sail to negotiate the icy winter sky and rising like spring song...in a cold sky that simultaneously holds the opposing flowing energies that move and shift positions, the wanton pattern that is the chaotic, evil spirit of catastrophe, the uncontrolled confusion of miasma that creates the malignant epidemic of pestilence, the plague of mysterious demons, the hot spring that rises up and emerges to create the aggregated mountain of wickedness, bewitching the people and living beings to harbor injustice and accept the rabbit warren of wrongs; and the upper emperor's imperial magic decree applies decapitation like spreading out a cloth, creating a flowering prosperity of enlightenment, sending down like falling leaves the writing of the five-elements' story, the red book of jade characters, the eight majestic dragons' writings, defending the barrier to the precious treasure, preserving the body and blessing the world, with its system of regulation and restraint to contain the robbing and plundering of time by calamity, the revolving wheel sent by the chief of Heaven to deposit, store, and preserve the Brahmanic Qi that pervasively reaches and fills up the collecting net of the myriad patterns that unfold and spread out; at the origin point, the guiding principle is at the head rope of the net that flows outward, evolving the performance of the scene, the winding unbroken chant that flows like a stream, the wheel of the 32 Heavens that turns, colorless, making its circuit as it revolves through the ten directions the dipper whirling like a lathe in successive spirals that sweep through the dustpan pattern of the winnowing basket in a circle of salvation for the five elements;

道藏輯要

三十五分總氣上元八景宴合氣入玄玄玄中太皇上帝高眞
泛景太霞噏詠洞章金眞朗郁流響雲營玉音橋氣靈風聚烟
紫虛鬱秀輔翼萬仙五氣混合自然成眞眞中有神太極元君
三天眞老大混尊神太一司化三五神官執符把籙保度靈眞
上遊上清出入華房八冥之內細微之中下鎭五嶽上安九天
中理五氣混合百神十轉迴靈萬氣齊仙五行邪怪斬滅無干
高明紫微流轉諸天掌世罪福與道同玄仙道貴生無量度人
炎炎五星飛天如輪下維九宮上開八門罪福禁戒宿命因緣
普受開度五行生身身得受生上間諸天之上各有生門
中有五行空洞之章眞王靈篇辭參高眞

...thirty five divisions assemble together the Qi of the upper origin, the eight scenes brought together in dark mysterious harmony like poetry in a fire, and the Qi enters the mystery within the mystery, so that at the center of the mystery the great emperor can ascend to the imperial palace of truth, bathed in the bright scene of the red tinged clouds, whistling the chant, the music of mind in the cavern, the chapter of golden truth clear and bright, green and lush like tree clusters, elegant and fragrant as it floats, circulates and spreads, the astronomical sound ringing out and resonating through the Heavenly township, the jade camps of clouds absorbing and assimilating the tones and their Qi, and the numinous spirit energy of the weather on the wind amassing into a purple smoke of bliss in the emptiness - dense, elegant, auxiliary clouds like wings at the sides of the ten thousand immortals, the five Qi united in a grand blended torrent, in a spontaneous and natural completion into perfect truth; at the center of truth there is divinity, the "Supreme Ultimate", the state of undifferentiated absolute and infinite potential, the oneness before duality, primitive order of the universe; three Heavens of eternal truth (past, present, and future) flow in an all-embracing torrent that honors divine spirit; the great unity takes charge of the transformation of "the three and the five", and divine spirit officers seize the charm and hold the jade talisman book of fortune, to protect and defend salvation with the numinous spirit energy of truth, ascending to roam in the upper clarity, exiting and entering the flower room; on the inside of the eight obscurities, the eight material offerings, the delicate and quiet, tiny profound center below is guarded by the golden truth of the five high peaks, ascending into the quiet contentment and peace of the nine Heavens....at the center the fundamental law ruling the rotating muddy chaos of the ocean of the five Qi are the hundred divine spirits, and the ten directions transform with the revolutions of the wheel of spiritual energy, evening out the myriad Qi for the immortals; the demonic strangeness within the five elements, cut off and left alone, had nothing to do with; the lofty bright purple profound flows and transforms, moving on through the various Heavens; with a slap from the hand the world's guilt is washed away into blessing and good fortune, so that it takes part in the Dao together with the profound mystery of the crimson chamber; the Daoist immortals' venerable pure life is boundless salvation, the burning, blazing five elements' stars flying through Heaven like a wheel the Daoist immortals' venerable pure life is boundless salvation, the burning, blazing five elements' stars flying through Heaven like a wheel to preserve and maintain Nine Temple Palace below, while above the eight gateways open out, and any wrongdoing in the blessing is forbidden and guarded against, restrained by the cave that is the constellations' halting-place, the lodge of night, where life's fate meets the cause that produces effects in another stage of existence, so that all receive, accept, and endure the universal teaching that opens out into salvation, the five elements giving birth to the body, the body obtaining and bearing pure life that ascends when it hears all the various Heavens, and all the various Heavens' ascensions existing in each and every pure life that goes through the doorway at the center where the five elements in the empty cavern's chapter of truth is ruled by the numinous energy of the spirit world, written into a ballad of phrases that is a gathering for the purpose of meditation, preaching, and worship, like a lofty star of truth.

第一化生五行飛空之音
無形無名
二儀分兮
大梵未開
位列五行
東青西素
五氣相循
各有主性
南丹北玄
元一中黃
此為道根
色質相連
上真仙聖
與道變遷
寶臺玉宮
碧山金門
運合真神
皆真五色
無量帝君
冥冥之中
紫蓋朱輪
分化億千
錦旆黃綬
息意冥一
隨化成形
飛空結仙
此道世莫知
超度三界
真王當普宣
神雩散萬里
金闕相輝鮮
飛神恍惚間
萬聖馳雲騎
世途念流轉
妙本晤所歸
使我常哀憐
何如向玄道
邪怪盡淪息
長居玉帝前

The first part: metamorphosis of life into the magic salvation, the five elements flying out from the emptiness with the beautiful tidings:

The Great Brahman, not yet opened out, without form, without name, until the "BOOM!" of release divided all into two - two modes, the two styles, YIN and YANG, sharing duties in the grand divine and positive event of becoming, with the five elements arrayed in a column like a train, pure and crystal clear, headed out to the five directions - the east, green like seedlings of grass under a blue sky, like mountain green water, the west, white and pure like raw silk, simple and unadorned, the south, cinnabar red like the blood, like fire, like the elixir of immortality, the north, black and mysterious like a dark and deep pit, silent and mysterious as Heaven, and the profound yellow origin of the center, holding together all the diverse mysteries, the five Qi interacting,

mutually teaching and learning from each other, following each other in accord like the hearts of stars, each one master of his own properties, ruler of his individual nature, and all taking part in the divine and positive mystery of transformation , twisting and turning in the river of Way; these became the fundamental root of the Dao. As the colors, qualities, and physical natures spun on the revolving wheel, up on the precious platform terrace of the Jade temple palace, in the blue green mountains that are the golden gate, the immortal sage of superior truth, boundless emperor gentleman, entered into the unseen world of the spirit realm, where the revolving wheel brings together and combines the true, invisible spirits, taking them into immortality,
the revolving fortune weaving them into a brocade flowing like water, like clouds containing the diverse mysteries, in a gently settled embroidery of ribbons and seals, the purple canopy over the vermilion wheel of Heaven as all truth flows within the beautiful stream of the five colors,

following along in accord and transforming into perfection through form and body, the thoughts and feelings resting and ceasing, the netherworlds of hearts and minds all turning into a deep unified obscurity, a pristine darkness; as the branching transformation flow of salvation penetrates into the million bottomless depths, guiding all in a saving flight of transcendence across the three borders of past, present, and future existence, flying out into the hollow void, out of the knots and bonds of false views and passions, and into immortality; in this world there are none who are not held within the Dao; the king of Reality undertakes the universal spreading of the proclamation, spirits in the sky enumerate the fates and destinies of the ten thousand villages; at the golden watchtower the sign appears of a shining martial force, fresh and bright, the flying spirits clearing a gap into minds of distraction, idleness opening the door out of confusion into clarity, the ten thousand sages like a flood of poetry, like teams of horses galloping across the clouds, into the world, singing on their way as they float and flow, wander and spread, circulate, move, and drift, revolve and transform, bringing the message of eternal compassion as we travel together into the ultimate Reality that is the mystery of the Dao, the profound, wonderful, mystical root that we go to meet, as we surrender and return into it, and all mysterious evils wash away, as the brush washes the moon in the ripples of a sentence, difficulty and mistake perishing like wavelets that perish when water is turned round and released, wavelets of annoyance and agitation, of disease and death extinguished in the ocean that washes over them, as the affairs of mind calm and settle, and the development of lofty righteousness comes home to dwell with the emperors of the Jade, where the boat comes to a stop, the shores of immortality.

第二斬滅五行邪怪之章

檢挍陰陽　運合元機　五行邪怪
五福之章　統部神官　三五將軍
青龍左列　白虎右當　佩服龍鎧
保合生精　華衣繡裙　玉冠青巾
天元太乙　帝司主兵　護衛世上

莫不傾摧
敷佑福祥　啟悟希夷　邪怪已消滅
五帝降靈威　護世過萬年　帝德日照熙
黃龍下中天　帝壽天所期
奏香綠烟飛　　　　　　　神霄空洞章

有邪必斬
有怪必摧

Second Part: The song of cutting off and extinguishing the five elements' mysterious evils:

After the great winding bend from Heaven's origin, the emperors had to take charge in order to control the military force of the soldiers on the road, and so created and composed a protecting guard, to defend and shelter both mind and body with an ever-flowing river of discipline, to restrain and escort in the twilight, guarding and defending as a form of hygiene for life that prevents sinking into the darkness of the earth, protecting with a barrier the secret treasure, like wrapping a baby in swaddling clothes, holding together the masses in a harmony like the reverent unity of a monastery, to defend the subtle vitality of all beings. Like a flower, wearing embroidered robes, with the jade crown of nature's green for a head covering, a green-blue dragon lined up on the left for the ceremony, a white tiger the guest on the right*,

(* a Daoist immortal is always pointed toward Southern Heaven, and so has the green of the west at this left shoulder and the white of the east at his right shoulder;)

the leader and teacher appears fully dressed and decorated to announce and spread the medicine of truth, the dragon that is the double edged sword of law, protecting all, with the blessings of the five elements and the five directions in its patterns, gathering and unifying all the members of the world in the Spirit Palace, with the "three and the five"** in command of the army,

[**the "three and the five" is the "three southern and five northern breaths", the ritual of taking in the 8 auspicious scenes every morning with deep breaths and keeping them in the storehouse-treasury-depository of the vitality, a form of "retentive contemplation" -"cún sī " 存思 , or "retentive visualization" - " cún jiàn" 存見. "Sān-Wǔ Hé Qì Jiǔ-Jiǔ Jié - The Three Southern and Five Northern Breaths harmonize the Qi." http://www.dztranslation.org/texts/vol-0131/daozang-0131-021b1.html]

carrying out the inspection of the military like a leader under a tree, standing in the wind with the spear of YIN and YANG, the revolving of Heaven bringing all into accord like poetry, the army and the families and even the horses joined together in prayer with the Prince of Original Principle. With the Five Elements' mysterious demons of confusion and depravity, there is no one who isn't inclined to fall into collapse with sadness and pain, in danger of being broken by the enemy; there are certainly unhealthy influences to be beheaded, there are certainly bewildering monsters to be trapped and conquered; applying Heaven's blessing and protection, taking cover in the shelter and asylum of divinity, brings good fortune and happiness, creating a cloud of auspicious Qi, and the soldiers are blessed by the omen, the mysterious evils already melted away, extinguished, scattered and annihilated by the wind of Heaven; the five emperors subdue and tame with the beauty of the wind and the majesty of light, their dignity and glory manifested in the power of the weather in paradise; the ever-flowing river of discipline protects the world, helping life get past errors, transgressions, going past humanity's natural mistakes and out into the kaleidoscope of eternity, the virtuous power of the emperors a bright and flourishing radiance, a bustling fire of ancient light overlooking revitalization, a jubilee of blessing developing vigorously and causing prosperity, training by the light and the music of the Way, the dragon culminating in midair above the diverse mysteries below, the emperors of longevity living in Heaven's rhythm, the spirits of the clear sky, above the clouds, inhabiting the vacuous cavity, seeing through, beyond the false and illusory nature of all existence, making their pledge, singing their song, wearing their flag, chanting their poetry, ringing their bell, writing their chapter, they memorialize the emperor's original meaning with their trend of righteousness, as they play out their performance of victory, that sweet smelling fragrance of green that rises and flies into Heaven like smoke.....

第三和合五行歸身契道歌曰

太虛立妙神　空洞幽无君　生於渺㳽中
造化標元根　淡漠居正性　返照滅邪氛
消魔怪害除　沖融和至眞　昭昭智惠鋒
戒戈化禾辜　五蜀妄能優　明輝華景形
佩服靈寶章　雲光煥爾身　玉符鎭肉景
龍虎纏胎嬰　水火金木交　混一宗皇靈
窺覬御絳闕　冥冥理百精　誰知年劫運
長保無翁齡　舞輪三界外　朝翔登九清

Third part: the harmony flame of the five elements, reverting and returning as a family into the body, singing a covenant with the Dao on Song Day:

In the great emptiness, the void of Heaven, the universe, the subtle, profound, mysterious Spirit, in the empty, vacuous cavity, the netherworld is not in charge. Pure life is born into the drama of the vast and vague sea of indifferentiation and boundlessness, a cloud of mystery blooming in the ancient river, an exquisite flower in the middle of the ten billion mile ditch,

荞 qiáo common mallow (Malva sinesis); variant of 蕎

漭 mǎng vast; expansive (of water);

ultimate Daoist immortal form of 澒蒙渺茫 "hong meng miao mang" - " the grand goose of wild unconscious in the vast and vague sea of indifferentiation and boundlessness" ("the undifferentiated, obscure and boundless", "the big concealment"), and the Daoist goal of boundless universal salvation;

nature's creation, the dawn of luck, a trembling chestnut sprouting from the tree like a muddy gem pregnant with good fortune, an impulsive sprout from the ancestral dragon growing out of the wooden tip, growing out of the original fundamental root; insipid, diluted, indifferent, cold, and weak, it's nature is to dwell in the right and correct, to return the shine of illumination that extinguishes the demonic miasma, an illumination in the fierce and funerary atmosphere that manages the condensate from the cloud of the improper and random disorder, the foul cloud of war, a sparkle and weep extinguishing the destroyer's bewildering mystery, a magic living poetry preventing calamity, washing away disturbance of body and mind in a flood of transformation that removes the brutal forces of evil from the steps of the palace, with a flow that faces toward the sun like a planet moving straight ahead in a mysterious surge, just a seedling surging upward, a cup of tea steeping in the empty chamber of mystery, with a far reaching peace, red mystery holding off the war carriage with its red waves, the overflowing red rain from the upwelling heart like an ice chisel that ends up melting and blending into harmony, the perfection of the profound truth, like the subtle and marvelous presence of a saint melting into the true reality of the immortals, learning to flow gracefully under the invisible load of the Qi, cutting down demons like bamboo, like an army that scolds and teaches the mob, extinguishing error with a shock of accusations and chastisement, the way the craftsmen that are the sun and moon carve the earth; the muddy impurities of the five are stilled and quieted into the security of good health, like a bear secluded in a cave and able to withstand the bottomless energy, the bright quiet that can withstand the interference of the greedy marsh, the smoky halo around the burning sun of enlightenment melting away in the flowery scene that is the physical form of body. Wearing the precious jade garment that is the numinous power of Heaven, the body is a cloud of brilliant light, lustrous with rejuvenation, both the mortal and the spiritual bodies, radiant; the weight and pressure of the surrounding jade charm guards and protects the scenery of the interior, in concentric layering shells of time, like gold covering a well, like a temple supervisor maintaining calm and order, like auspicious stars covering mountains, dragon and tiger winding to wrap around the flowering embryo, nourishing and cultivating the development of the exquisite infant, water, fire, metal, wood, and the deep darkness of earth, mixing together into one, following the model of the emperors' primal spiritual energy; the majestic and towering imposing sway of the emperors' respect-inspiring, dignified authoritative virtue drives the royal wheel that controls the long river carrying along the world, carriage and horse without fear of all the coasts of static, as they fiercely defend the royal street that leads to the Purple-Red Main gate of the Emperors' Palace, high, distant, and Primordial, the home of the five gods; the lofty and invisible intrinsic order, ruling principle of the cosmos that manages the essence of the stars - who can reject or escape the turning of its wheel? The forever-defended, inexhaustible wisdom of the dreaming emperors of universal spirit, that grows in leaning knots and slowly flowing tears, whose evening dance is the turning of the wheel, whose external manifestation is the three borders of past, present, and future existence that ripens in the soaring of time, ascending, guided by the imperial pilot, through the cloud gate into the quiet clarity of Heaven.

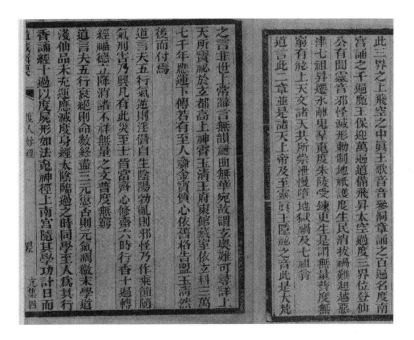

Flying above these three borders to win the beyond, True Ruler, King of the Real - sings tone on tone of the tidings, in a practice of reflection, meditation, and worship, to join with the simplicity of the cavern, in exploration, understanding, and release, reciting the chapter's universe of names for salvation in the Southern Temple Palace, the recitation of the thousand devils that reside everywhere is a great protection to guard the barriers, the emperor's mountain stick a protection that trains the world into righteousness and preservation; to face and to welcome the "WAN BIAN DAO" - the "10,000 everywheres" Dao - in preparation to rise and to ascend in fullness and peace like the sunrise into the Great Emptiness, the Great Vacant Vacuity, into the Spirit above illusory existence, the abstraction without relativity, transgression and error fallen away into the Past, in a celebration of crossing over, the festival of salvation that reaches the other shore, beyond the three borders of Past,

Present, and Future Existence, stepping into the ripening that attains the seat of immortality, awakening into the secret truth of the ancestors and kings that exists when hearing the efficacious spirit sounds that extinguish and defeat the mysterious evils, blowing out the bewildering flame that leads toward error and illness; the body's form absorbing the powerful imperial commands to simmer in regulation and restraint, while reverent earth spirits protect the inner self as well as the body, saving the life of the people, the elder brother of poetry melting and wiping away misfortune, pulling up disaster and calamity by the roots, leaping over distress to pass into bliss, crossing over beyond the prison of evil that tries to trap the Qi, riding the ferry of salvation to the seven founding ancestors in a peaceful ascent that swims in the eternally flowing brightness of immortality, leaving behind the flock of hungry ghosts and scattered wandering dreams, and crossing over to the vermilion mountains and rose sky of the fairy realm, to receive-accept-endure the refinement, the training that holds the wind of experience contained within to receive the blessings of Heaven and earth, standing in the middle of the boat with both hands open to bear, and going further, into pure life; this is truly called the boundless and inexhaustible universal salvation, the mysterious secret of ascending into Heaven, all the diverse kinds intersecting and coming together in pious worship and sacrifice, hands folded together under Heaven in the lofty place of honor, full of reverence, pragmatically dismissing evil, flying away from pride/ laziness/arrogance like mist escaping from a vent, not falling into the earth prisons of suffering, but released from disaster, misfortune, and calamity and reaching upward to achieve the place of the seven elderly patriarchs.

The Dao says these two sections have the spiritual power to reach up to and achieve the diverse Emperors in the upper Heavens, where the true king keeps hidden the secret of the divine tidings, the Great Brahman's words, not of the world or of the present epoch, but of the upper and eternal, poetic speech made without rhyme, a beautiful and elegant display like a deer in the wind, peaceful under the sun and moon, an artful song like a bending river, not wasteful or ornate but bending gracefully, smoothly, and mildly in subtle twists like grass in the breeze, in order to describe and explain the mystery within the mystery, the deep and profound secret of the universe, able to fathom the details of the upper reaches of the Heavens, the place of the secret hidden mystery, the profound lofty metropolis, the spirit above the rainclouds and the rainbow of night, the great kingdom of the Jade Clarity, the Eastern Palace Embassy schoolroom, the storehouse-treasury-depository abode, the heart that all depend on, learn from, and comply with, the dark mystery field, the three myriad seven thousand years we reflect and respond to, the revolving wheel of fortune that tutors everything below, painting all with justice, that counsels and guides, the structure of the imperial teacher, like a house for mankind that offers a nurturing shell of training, golden pearls in a sea of wisdom, the ancient heart to be followed along with, the frame and pattern worn with age that informs with Jade announcement, the persuasive explanation that is an anti-poison, that correctly aligns us with the Jade Clarity, and afterward hands down and delivers the flying corrective absence.

The Dao says a man who goes against the Qi of the five elements, who turns against the flow of the stream in deterioration, or follows an inverse channel contrary to the elders of the mind into a vortex, like a flow spinning into an eddy, creates a pattern of depraved excess and oversteps the guidelines like a pirate splashing in the chaos of transgression, arrogating beyond home and habitat, shooting like a comet beyond one's own pure life and its YIN and Yang balance, pushing like a smoke of confusion and disorder against the guiding walls of Heaven's pattern, like a cloud rising up into the evil mystery of demons; therefore a vehicle of writings is composed to connect compliance with the Qi to a method that restricts people from doing harm, and protecting from injury, so that the lives of all can be allowed to flourish and prosper, and the scourge of disaster and calamity and personal misfortune can be dispelled by the power that arrives at perfection above the dark dirt of the earth, everyone wrapped in a shell of prolonged and eternal nurturing that regards all as equal, hearts cultivating abstinence and mending error with fasts, the practice into the late hours rising like fragrance into the universe everywhere, to float, flow, wander, spread, circulate, move drift, revolve, and transform, the Jade Scriptures of blessing, happiness, and moral virtue, of kindhearted love and benevolent goodwill, direct and warm, strong and righteous, becoming established to eliminate all the diverse kinds of inauspicious omens, in writing of boundlessness and inexhaustible universal salvation.

The Dao says a man whose standards descend and decrease progressively away from the wind of the five elements, withering in slack and sluggish fatigue, cuts short the positive flow of the Qi that creates the pattern of his destiny, pushing it several steps toward its end in death, the Qi of the three origins (Heaven's, earth's, and man's) wilting in injury like a broken wing, shrinking in atrophy into a slight and withered broken twig that quickly turns to dust, the study and understanding of the Dao only shallow and superficial while the flow of the current beneath washes the twig away, the highest level of immortality not yet fulfilled, the chorus not finished, the bell tone of fullness not yet struck, the revolving wheel of fortune answered with an extinguishing of the salvation of the body and life; in contrast to this fate the scripture's greatest hidden Yin energies approach with kindness before the time of departure with an invitation to study and learn to reach the mystery, and for man to become his element, his ideal action, fragrant like incense as he sings the scriptures and crosses over past transgressions in order to save himself from becoming a corps, his body following the powerful method, a wizard flower soul on the narrow track of the spirit path, the cloud trail that man can walk but cattle cars cannot travel, a path tangent to the habitat, to the upper Southern Palace where he goes in compliance with his learning, achieving the meritorious accomplishment through strength and earnest effort, and arriving at the place where his days are yet not counted.

得更生轉輪不惑便得神仙道言五行之氣出為邪怪則致天地運終星宿錯度日月失明四時失度陰陽不調國界不寧兵火時起疫毒流行兆民死傷師友命過皆當修齋行香誦經則五行邪怪之鬼閒經鎮呼其姓名稱說根本因緣之狀叩首請命永不敢干經隱妙道及以真符無不禳却也夫齋戒誦經功德甚重上消天災斬滅邪怪保鎮帝王下禳害以度兆民生死受賴其福難勝故曰無量普度天人

"On Obtaining the changing experience of life, that revolves and transforms, riding the turning of the wheels without illusion or concern, gently, informally and easily, and obtaining spirit immortality":

Daoism says that the five elements go forth to (deal with) the demonic, nefarious, evil, unhealthy, mysterious and bewildering spirits, and to divert them, to send, devote and deliver Heaven and earth in the revolving wheel, to carry them forward in their migration like a ship through the seas of fortune, and to resettle them at the end like a star lodged in the constellations of the night, all mistakes and wrongs ground and polished into the gold of salvation - enlightenment - wholeness, ferried across the waves of time like a boat by a guide; the lost brightness of the sun and moon and the four seasons is a loss to that ferry of saving, Yin and Yang not harmonized, not controlled and tuned in their song, their home land, the home force, not in repose, not settled, the fire of war, bodies with internal heat, a time of uprising for epidemics of poison, omen of death for the multitudes, when they've gone past their yang teacher, that friend of destiny and fate, passing their limits as passing the shore and into an ocean, fallen into that ocean of transgression; all and each undertakes the mending, the cultivation, teaching the practice, putting in order by fasting, abstinence, and purification practices, teaching the thoughts, words, and deeds that move toward perfection, the sweet smelling incense and the recitation of the scriptures; from the cloud of law and the rainstorm of language, the five elements cause the ghosts and demons of nefarious mystery to be heard and sniffed at in the scriptures, so that they can be guarded against, suppressed by the weight and pressure of the gold, restrained and governed, limited and bound when the "bang!" of their names are noted, as they are called and invoked into the weight of the balanced steelyard, where speech is used to explain the solution and release into joy; the fundamental root and stem is the shape of the cause that produces effects in another stage of existence, knocking the door, striking the wolf, leading the song of enlightenment, beginning the building of the capital city, requesting and inviting fate to flow like an unceasing river of poetry, the wind of longevity extending time and space, never daring to break from integrity, not opposed to the scriptures in any way, that concealed incomparable mystery, subtle and profound, with deep purpose, the wonderful speech of the Dao that leads to release and enlightenment, reaching by means of a talisman of truth, a mysterious instrument, an amulet that contains everything, a prayer of sacrifice to avoid calamity, a festival of Qi as assertive as a star launched against the dangers of the calendar, throwing its devils of the gaps into confusion.

The sage fasts in reverent abstinence to guard the boundaries and limits of the journey as he departs on the road, singing the scriptures, knowing self-alert poems with the power of virtue, their heavy repetition rising up and disappearing into Heaven, like smoke vanishing into the sky, a medicine that melts away and disperses poisons, disaster and calamity cut off and extinguished like a flame by the ocean of Heaven, as the unhealthy influences and strange mysterious disorder disappears into emptiness like clouds scattered into clarity; the sage defends and protects, with his mountain stick wielding the pressure and weight of Heaven like a monarch over the world below, his prayer and sacrifice averting disaster, eliminating plagues, his rituals driving assertive Qi against fierce traveling devils of danger and harm and throwing them into confusion, his powerful solution driving away the thick toxic and bitter poison of rebellion that threatens to disturb, in order to save, in order to cross to the shore of liberation; as the omens of life and death are received and endured by the multitudes, their good fortune and blessing is dependent upon their following and walking along the difficult path of victory, with all its beauty and wonder, which is the intention of the boundless universal salvation by Heaven for mankind;

道言凡有是經能爲天地帝主兆民行是功德有災之日發心修齋燒香誦經十過皆諸天記名萬神侍衞右別至人尅得爲聖君金闕之臣諸天記人功過毫分無失天中眞王亦保擧衞身得道者乃當洞明至言也

諸天中大梵隱語無量音　道君譔

元始靈書中篇

The Dao says that the scriptures contain the cinnabar remedy that is capable of showing Heaven as the great monarch over the earth, the omen for the road of the people's thoughts, words, and deeds, the right merit and virtue of their hearts and minds radiating fortune, and launching a pre-emptive strike against disaster, sprouting the growth that flows through generations, the practice of cultivation, fasting, and the heat from the fires of sacrifice a sweet smelling offering like incense, like ten recitations of the scriptures of diverse kinds flowing into Heaven, sacrifices made with Heaven in mind; the ten-thousand spirits attending to guard and protect like a garrison at an outpost in the twilight, with the power of the right hand separating, differentiating and distinguishing in the darkness like the lines cracking on the back of a turtle shell, so that man will be able to shoulder the responsibility of overthrowing the clouds of darkness, of restraining the elephant, to obtain the victory, the becoming of holiness and saintly character; the ideal man is a king of merit, on the other side of knowing, like a sheep who hears the door, the golden vacant watchtower's minister with square pupils upright as the arrow in a bow, [glyph] and with Heaven in mind, his achievement of strength crossing over past error and into life, not the slightest thing missed, not a cent not a mustard seed lost, in the effort to hit the mark of Heaven;

-----

a real king who also protects others like a father carrying children on his back, holding them up so their lives can obtain the Dao, someone who undertakes to bear the future selflessly, whose bright perfect speech is like a bell ringing out in the empty cavern, all of Heaven, the Great Brahman of mystic devotion and sacred learning, the substratum and support of all, hidden within his words, within the boundless tidings; the Dao's king compiles and composes with the original primal spirit energy, while writing his book on the bamboo slips.

"walking the road that is difficult"

行路難

xíng　lǔ　nàn

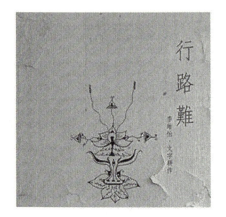

- by the painter Zhu Da, who often painted the eyes looking up; and in this fish, the square eyes, as in the legend of Daoist immortals being recognizable by the square iris

東方八天　律角冥外　祺羅屈丹
橙俞离瓊　雲霏瑤閬　利逸謹慧
妙穎楚僅　偃管生記　珠煥陽甫
叅鐸鵠房　巒格燕盞　冒德施隨
符梁熙眛　華光撐匱　嬰璟何容
青鄙洛汶
枳墩陸會

The Eastern Eight Heavens

Like orange holes in space, they are the opportunity for beginning; consent, permission, wearing emptiness, distant, separate points like oranges on branches, like rare mythical beasts, strange and elegant, the fire, the original grass, in the beautiful, exquisite jade,

they lead with discipline, with the constraints of poetic beauty, arbiters of all measurement, in an ancient theatre that is the alchemy chamber, operating outside the darkness of the netherworld,

together they form the auspicious net, favorably disposed, bright, encouraging, and lucky - the net of moon and stars that brings forth the cinnabar;

profound, subtle, and mysterious, the clever points like heads of grain, clear, distinct brambles that both punish and clear, like medicine, just a simple cure,

a cloud of snow within the precious green crystal, forming a barrier, impassable, a doorway closing off a compartment,

A sharp and beneficial escape of cautious and sincere discernment, the leisurely wisdom,

the flashing truth that is the counsel of the golden constellations, the meditating gathering to explore and understand, ringing like bells that gather the quail into the monastery;

stopped in the weir, dazzled in the florescence of the celestial camp the confusion of the cities finds a base camp and gives birth to pure life under the sign that remembers, and foretells;

the Heavenly truth of the milky white pearls, burning brilliantly, like flowers, the lustrous poetry of Heaven, the YANG forming "pellets" layer by layer, in a distance barely scratched,

a talisman or charm that is a bridge, like wood supported across water, the illumination that is the stars, the faint touch of white, the bright shining transformation a latent force collected inside within the mountain range of peaks, is a pattern to be studied exhaustively, like a swallow's hollow, a vessel like a dish to finish, to sit before and practice utmost pervasion in, the empty righteous extension;

daring to send out like smoke the virtue that carries out compliance and accord,

the blue green, ancient rustic river of the heart

a flower that shines the ray, that picks out, differentiates, and discriminates, picking the true food from the dish, emptying the best from the cabinet;

the white jade book that wraps around the infant, an ancient ring, an infinite loop that encircles, the forbearance and countenance that allows what?

the medicine of the oranges is the pillar of the gate, leading to the shore, where we assemble, communicate, and comprehend....

南方八天

曖曨奎常　九暄柏枚　漾朗冀沣
琢英明住　卜處蠶曬　上抔驛催
救溢秉琅　圖倨金夷　渺歷定簿
怛佑慈理　洎浦牛童　加那彦東
梵珞祕思　以龍伍轅　覿綿炳懟
金庭蕭仙

The Southern Eight Heavens

In the dim twilight before dawn, the KUI constellation shines into eternity, like nine warm and genial cedar tree trunks;

the long frozen river carries along, clear and bright, containing the diverse mysteries in its ancient waters, polishing the gems of outstanding brightness and allowing them to flow naturally in their revolving course;

thinking and anxiety used up, exhausted and empty, divining by the brilliant and shining constellations, at the hill the great commander urges on the post horses;

The saving flow of the river grasps the clean and white tinkling jade; the map, the seal, of revolving, embracing wholeness, aloof, extinguishes the gold;

the vast and expansive calendar fixed and determined in its calculation, a fixed and constant protection, with compassion and mercy as its inner principle;

along the shore by the brook, the young child rides the bull playing the flute, adding on the beautiful, elegant, refinement in the east, as the dragon pulls the powerful cart that rolls across the sky;

Face to face with the bright, luminous, glorious cotton, soft and continuous like silk floss, powerful like a sound of tears from the heart, the gold courtyard is a luxuriant growing flower for the immortal.

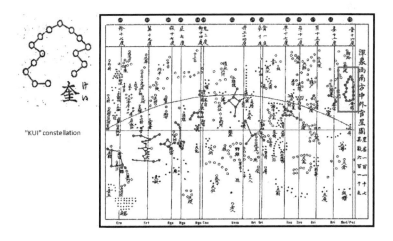

"KUI" constellation

Western Eight Heavens

The metal from the sun, spun like pottery, woven like silk, like a DNA helix, into a historical record, can be slowed down, prolonged, delayed, remaining in the cavern, preserving the lush field, to open up and initiate the awakening, like a proclamation;

In the role of the stars in their course, from out of the east, into the void, rapid universal pervasion flows in a venerated torrent;

Beckoning at the fixed times the pure, simple, miniature profundities, the beneficial increase of the numerous, pure, plain, natural white elements in the rice vessel, each one complete and whole,

Soaring, prancing, rising, and then vacating;

we can grasp them for a moment, then allow them to carry on, as they spread forward in their proclamation, along the sincere and true road, smoothly progressing, prosperous, clever, full of heart,

they help us to cross over the netherworld with their deep pools of profound joy, interlocking the country with a teacher, a model that leads by making circuits, turning and revolving over that draining creek that cuts through the valley;

Empty and lonesome, very few achieve and make it back to the origin, so, announcing to ordinary people who are uncertain, with a force like fists,

into the self-defeating limits of the demon's pond,

to rouse, restore, vibrate, and resonate, to raise up the spirit with its writings, like spirit entering through a door in a bamboo weir over the pond, coming down from the clean and white tinkling jade in the sky, to implore, to request,

Chinese poetry like an elder brother, a cool desert, indifferent, a sage, a hero, to offer people strength, the virtue to become prosperous, via its quotations and allusions, the spiritual energy blowing through full of sincerity, wholeness, to complete the spirit and end the fear.

北方八天

列晤壹定　耿澄微菜　鑑萌資條

陽璉印部　贍但瓊拂　拯紀盈剔　仙潭碧洙

撰慈窺冥　番波氏石　粲調持屏

友句肆亭　聿琳序演

閬廛靚沭　洋略扁飛　雷族咸匡

蹟眞皇微

The Northern Eight Heavens

An arrangement lined up to provide a clear explanation that is sincere, fixed, and determined,

the brightness clarifying the tiny and profound lush grasses,

like viewing a reflection in a mirror, of buds and sprouts in wealth and plenty in a long strip,

a seal engraved with YANG, a vessel marked with carved ideas together in a group of volumes;

Only lightly grazing like a soft breeze on the inner container of beautiful exquisite jade,

rescuing and saving the woven order of the chronicle, picking off just enough from the full dish, selecting out from the surplus,

compiling and composing with kind and loving affection a sneaking glance into profound secret invisible darkness;

As the rippling waves on the outside turn, the foundation is inscribed;

The immortal in the great deep pool of blue-green swims as if in a river of perpetual dawn;

Closed off as if in the small box of a friendly phrase, the very best, unrestrained,

the precious fairy residence is an introduction, the introductory preface that develops into an expounded sermon like an exquisitely performed play,

with bright and polished conversation like brilliant flowers, regulating, tuning, harmonizing, to preserve the barrier, the screen of the retreat, where one lives in seclusion, where breath is suppressed, where the world is removed and hidden, abandoned,

in a hidden place of beautiful flowing abundance, luxuriant, in the vast ocean outlined by the inscribed tablet's flight,

a thunder that calls all and each into harmony on the banks;

the marks indicating the true emperor, tiny and abstruse, yet profound.

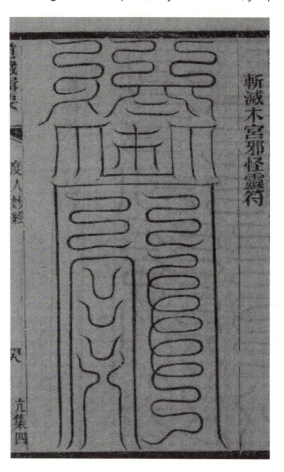

斬滅木宮邪怪靈符

"punishing and extinguishing the WOOD temple palace mysterious demons efficacious numinous spirit energy charm"

斬滅火宮邪怪靈符

"punishing and extinguishing the FIRE temple palace mysterious demons efficacious numinous spirit energy charm"

斬滅土宮邪怪靈符
"punishing and extinguishing the EARTH temple palace mysterious demons efficacious numinous spirit energy charm"

斬滅金宮邪怪靈符

"punishing and extinguishing the METAL temple palace mysterious demons efficacious numinous spirit energy charm"

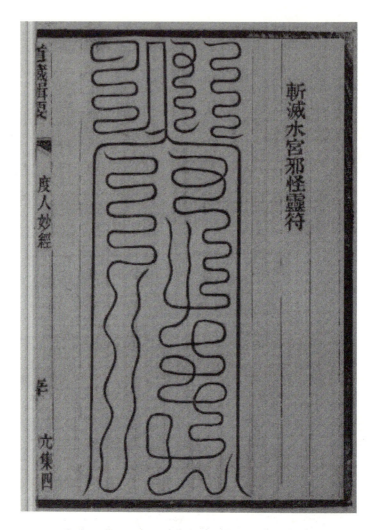

斬滅水宮邪怪靈符

"punishing and extinguishing the WATER temple palace mysterious demons efficacious numinous spirit energy charm"

Made in the USA
Columbia, SC
16 April 2021